W9-BHX-400

ADVENTURES

with

God

missionary life of
David & Georgina Solt

Lois Solt Emr Blackwell
forward by Luis Palau

Dedication

I especially want to thank my parents for their example of showing Jesus' love in many areas of their lives. This book is written in their honor. I am also grateful to my grandparents, Jacob and Lillian Solt, who saved many letters from my parents, from the 1930s to the 1970s, letters that provided much of the history shared in this amazing life of adventure with God.

Acknowledgements

A special thanks to Jerry Gramckow and Terri Morris for their invaluable help in getting this book completed.

Foreword
By Dr. Luis Palau

Dr. David Solt and I became good friends on the mission field, way back in the sixties and seventies. He was an outstanding missionary who was creative and who pioneered outreach to Latin America on radio. He started radio stations throughout Central America and in several other nations. I am convinced that because of David Solt's ministry, literally, without exaggeration, millions of Spanish-speaking people lost their prejudice against the Gospel, as explained in the New Testament, and surrendered their lives to Jesus Christ. I'm also convinced that many people—who formerly persecuted believers for their faith in the Bible as the Word of God and the authority for life and conduct—dropped their persecution because of listening to Godly Christian programs that David Solt purposefully aired across much of Latin America.

David Solt is also a very humble servant of Jesus Christ. To spread the Good News, he would literally do just about anything. He lived in areas of Mexico that were not easy at the time, and he and Georgina ministered joyfully. I remember him showing evangelistic movies in villages and towns to anyone who would stop and listen to the Good News Gospel.

David never abandons a friend. Once you are his friend, you are really his friend—forever. He's the kind of man you can talk to; he will do anything for you if you possibly can. Nothing was ever too big a request for David. He helped us in many evangelistic campaigns with sound, with projections, and with anything that needed to be done.

Latin America has been blessed by the presence of David Solt and his wonderful family. They have left the perfume of Christ, as in 2 Corinthians 2:14: *"But thanks be to God, who always leads us in triumphal procession in Christ and through us spreads everywhere the fragrance of the knowledge of Him."* Newer generations likely have no idea how that sweet smell of the gospel reached their land. But David Solt knows. So does God.

I delight to tell about David Solt because he is a great example to all of us.

Introduction

My parents were never ones to shy away from an adventure. So it wasn't much of a surprise to any of their Costa Rican friends when Senor Solt volunteered to pedal his bicycle through downtown San Jose on that pleasant spring day in 1948. Few civilians dared to venture into the mayhem that marked the brief but violent Costa Rican revolution that had begun a few weeks prior—but someone had to get to the post office to fetch the mail. With bullets whizzing through the air and lodging in trees, cars, walls, or, on occasion, vulnerable human flesh and organs, Dad pedaled on, peacefully confident that God would not allow his premature departure. After all, God had called David Solt to proclaim His gospel to the Costa Rican people—not to die from a stray bullet. Of that he was certain. But David Solt had one more reason to trust that God would spare him: his wife, Georgina, was seven months pregnant with their first child—me.

Dad did survive that bike ride, and over the next six decades, with his wife faithfully at his side, he continued his work of building radio towers and proclaiming the gospel via the airwaves—and through personal friendships with the Latin American people they both dearly loved. He was present for my birth at La Clinica Biblica. And over the next several years he and Mom enjoyed the arrival of five more Solt children to add extra spice to their Latin American missionary adventures. Throughout those decades, we Solts traveled tens of thousands of miles—mostly over U.S. highways and poorly paved or unpaved Latin American roads. We had some close calls on dangerous mountain roads. On many occasions we prayed our way through routine—and sometimes violent—Central American earthquakes. We endured some wicked weather, slithering snakes, voracious tropical insects, and the typical illnesses and injuries that mark everyday life in this fallen world. We're grateful for the life God gave us; we wouldn't trade it for anything.

Dad and Mom are long since retired, and before too long God will do what no stray revolutionary bullet or menacing earthquake was able to do: He will end their life on earth and take them home to Himself. That's why my siblings and I felt the need to share their amazing story now. We hope that as you read it you will enjoy at least a small measure of the joy we felt as children of these two precious Christian missionaries—David and Georgina Solt.

-   Lois Solt Emr Blackwell

Chapter One

How Did We Get Here?

CR

Only a week prior, two men in a new truck had failed to properly negotiate the hairpin turn we now faced; they had rolled helplessly to their deaths at the bottom of the rocky ravine, more than 100 feet below. Now we, a family of eight, including children from age fourteen (me) down to a nineteen-month-old baby, were about to attempt this most treacherous part of Guatemala's infamous "El Tapon" (The Cork)—with Mom driving a station wagon loaded to the roof with kids and supplies, and Dad following behind in a pickup truck—hauling a thirty-six-foot travel trailer!

How in the world did we get here? At various moments along our 4,000-mile journey in the spring of 1962, I think each of us quietly asked that question—at least those of us who were old enough to contemplate such thoughts. Rather than succumb to an Israel-in-the-desert moment, we prayed: "Dear Father, we know you brought us here so that we might continue on to El Salvador in order to build a radio station to declare your Word to the Salvadorian people. You did not bring us all the way out here just to die. Father, we ask for your hand to guide our vehicles around this turn and to uphold us should we start to fall."

Notice the rocks piled up at the turn.

We prayed, we placed our trust in God ... but we still had work to do. God promises to be with us, but He never promised to do everything for us. The ground directly below the turn sloped fairly gradually, so we were thankful that two men who had passed us in their Jeep, just before, on a wider stretch of the road, had carefully piled rocks in the sloping crux of the turn, widening the road at that crucial point.

The station wagon carrying mother and kids got through easily, without testing the makeshift road expansion. It was readily apparent that the truck and trailer would not fare so well. The question was: If—or, more likely, when—the tires pass over the loose rocks, will the rocks hold or will they give way—along with the vehicles and anyone inside? That possibility must have prompted Dad's precaution of placing a cookie can between the door and the door frame before he attempted the delicate maneuver around the rigid bend—solo. If the truck or the trailer began sliding down the cliff, he wouldn't need the extra second or two required to open the door—he'd bail out (onto solid ground, we hoped) as most of our belongings tumbled down to oblivion.

Inching along

So the process continued, with a large gravel truck chained up and pulling our pickup very gradually as Dad would hop inside and give the signal to the gravel truck driver. They'd move a foot or two—or sometimes just inches—and we'd all pray as some of the rocks built up in the crux loosened and then tumbled away. Then Dad would get out and crawl back under the trailer and jack it up, then run back to the truck, give the signal, and start the process yet again. The process was both tedious and terrifying.

Some of my younger siblings probably didn't fully comprehend the gravity of our situation, but I was fourteen at the time—I understood that my father was risking not only our family's financial well being, he was risking his life. But such peril was nothing new to Dad—or to Mom either, for that matter. By this point in their lives they'd been missionaries for more than fifteen years. Christian missionaries have, historically, risked property, life, and limb to take the gospel to those who've never heard its glorious, soul-saving message; my parents understood the risks when they

Driving through El Tapon was treacherous.

answered the call.

Before long, a large delivery truck rumbled up the ravine and its driver found the Solt family vehicles blocking his way. If he wanted to continue, he'd have to help us get through. So now—with his truck pushing from behind, the gravel truck pulling from the front, and Mom praying somewhat nervously as she and we children watched with anticipation—Dad carefully nudged the gas pedal and trusted God to get him through. For a few minutes the procedure appeared to be approaching the point of failure—and in this case failure might mean disaster. But, held up by God, the trucks powered through, and after a three-hour-long ordeal, the Solt family resumed its journey down El Tapon to El Salvador.

§

In an era of superhighways, powerful fuel-injected engines, and nearly flat-proof steel-belted tires, few are likely to appreciate the frequent annoyances we endured in our missions travels— flat tires, overheated engines, and a trailer door that didn't want to stay shut—as well as the sometimes death-defying adventures like the hairpin turn along El Tapon back in 1962.

Preparing to leave

My parents had no death wish, no desire to place their children in harm's way, but they did have a resolute commitment to follow the Lord wherever He led them. If doing so presented some risks … well that's just part of the adventure of being a true disciple of the God who said He would never leave nor forsake His people.

David Solt

My father, David Charles Solt, was born to devoted Christian parents, March 17, 1926, in Allentown, Pennsylvania. If you know anything about American history, then you know that Dad picked a rough time to be born. Americans were still living the high life of the "roaring twenties," but in three-and-a-half years America—and soon much of the world—would plunge from the high life into the Great Depression. When the depression hit, unemployment skyrocketed, and Jacob Solt, Dad's father, who was a machinist for Bethlehem Steel, didn't escape. Fortunately, he and his wife, Lillian, had a large house and were able to garner some income by taking in boarders.

Because the Solt Sr. home was just a few blocks from the Allentown

Dad and Uncle Paul were handsome boys, here sitting on their parents' laps.

Hospital, which had a nursing school, many of my grandparents' boarders were nursing students—a fact that might have played at least a small part in influencing first me and then my sisters Lillian and Liz to become nurses.

Dad's parents were devout believers who instilled in their two sons the deep Christian faith that had served them so well. The Solt family attended a nearby General Conference Mennonite church. In addition to taking their two sons to Sunday school and church, the elder Solts also sent them to church camps. But the training went even beyond that: the young brothers also attended Luther League classes at a nearby Lutheran church.

When Dad was just ten years old, and he and his younger brother, Paul, were at a Baptist Bible camp in Wescosville, Pennsylvania, Dad experienced the relief of having his sins forgiven and the glory of new birth in Christ.

Dad's grandfather on his mother's side, Irvin Walp, was a photographer. In 1920, Great Grandpa Irvin, commonly called I.R., bought Conrad Photo Studio in Meyersdale, Pennsylvania, where a family of Italian immigrants had settled some years prior.

Georgina DiValentino

I.R., like his children and grandchildren, was a devout, born-again Christian who had no qualms about sharing his faith. So when I.R. hired several Italian Roman Catholic sisters—the DiValentinos—to clean his studio, they had little choice but to listen to their employer's testimony of salvation by faith in Jesus' atonement for his sins.

I.R. Walp was a devout Christian.

Because the seven sisters and their brother lived on a farm that provided ample backgrounds for photographs, I.R. began to spend even more time with the DiValentino family; and even there on the farm, he brought his Bible and witnessed to all the family members.

In 1941, Georgina, born November 12, 1923, and the youngest of the DiValentino girls, graduated from high school and wanted to find a job that would get her off the farm. Despite her concern about having to endure Mr. I.R.'s incessant witnessing, she applied to work full time at the studio. I.R. hired her as his assistant, which meant she had to learn several new photography-related skills, including mixing the film-developing chemicals.

I.R.'s relentless witnessing was making some headway—Georgina was listening; she even began to read the Bible I.R. gave her. On Sundays, the family continued to attend the Roman Catholic Church, but after mass the sisters would carry their Bibles—hidden in newspapers lest their priest see them with the forbidden book—to I.R.'s studio for Bible study.

Not long after that, Frances, the

The DiValentino family posed for a photo on the farm.

oldest of the DiValentino girls, lost her husband in a traffic accident. At the funeral, held in the Catholic Church, the priest gave, as Georgina would later recall, "no hope for the living or the dead." Young Georgina felt compelled to write a letter to the priest, witnessing to what the Bible taught. The pupil had become a teacher. Georgina said, "My boss, I.R., was so pleased with what I had written that he gave me a leather-bound Bible."

When it became clear that the DiValentinos were leaving the Catholic Church, the priest came by to talk about the family's decision. The sisters began to discuss Bible passages, and the priest appeared befuddled—he couldn't locate the passages in his Bible! Georgina's break with the Catholic Church, and then with the ways of the world, was soon finalized.

Georgina, who'd never before enjoyed reading, soon became an avid reader—particularly of her Bible. As she read 2 Corinthians 5:17—"Therefore if any man be in Christ, he is a new creature; old things are passed away; behold, all things are become new"—she understood why she'd lost her desire for the things of the world: she was a new person, just as I.R. talked about. But her new life meant estrangement from many of her old friends—she now had little in common with them.

Georgina was an accomplished violinist.

When Georgina spoke to I.R. of her resultant feelings of isolation, he offered to buy her a ticket to visit Moody Bible Institute in Chicago over Christmas vacation. With her parent's permission, young Georgina caught a train, alone, to visit Moody and met many young students who shared her love of God and the Bible. She wanted to get the formal Bible training that Moody offered, but Chicago was far from Meyersdale. She soon learned that a similar institute, Philadelphia School of the Bible (PSB), was much closer, in Philadelphia.

So, not long after that, when I.R. was preparing to retire, and he offered to turn the photography business over to Georgina, she faced a decision that many would consider to be on the level of a dilemma: Would she accept the role of running a successful photography business offered by her mentor or would she follow her spirit, calling her to biblical ministry?

The decision wasn't difficult; Georgina was certain God was calling her to study His Word—she had to follow His leading. So did her sister Gloria. Together, on September 8, 1944, the sisters stashed their trunk and their cardboard boxes loaded with their belongings aboard a train bound for Philadelphia.

"Told You So"

Georgina and I.R.'s grandson David had been friends for years, but nothing more than that—after all, she was three years older than the ever energetic boy. Even so, her sisters had once proclaimed, prophetically as it turned out, "You're going to fall in love with David!" At the time, she protested; she had another boyfriend. But, even during those years of David's precocious youth, his affection for Georgina began to show through as he regularly looked for opportunities to spend time with her.

As Georgina began her second year at PSB, David began his first year at Swarthmore College, where he studied hard, played some second-string football, and played trumpet and French Horn in the marching band. Swarthmore, not surprisingly, is near enough to PSB that the two could spend their weekends together. They spent many of those weekends back in Allentown, with David's parents and I.R., who had moved in with them.

Then, on a visit to the DiValentino home in Meyersdale, as Georgina played the piano softly in the neighboring room, near enough to overhear the nearby conversation, David asked her father for permission to marry his daughter. With permission granted, the Solt family adventure was about to launch.

David and Georgina posed in 1946.

10

Chapter Two

Mr. and Mrs. Solt

CR

When David Solt, still a student at Swarthmore, showed up at PSB one autumn evening in 1945 to place an engagement ring on Georgina's finger, the event didn't go as smoothly as he'd planned. The PSB dorms were typical row houses, packed together in a fashion much like today's apartment buildings, so it wasn't easy for David to find an isolated—much less romantic—spot to present the ring to his beloved. Eventually they found a dark spot near a corner of the building. David pulled out the ring and placed it on the finger of the excited Georgina. They hugged as they expressed their undying love for one another—and at that moment who should drive around the corner and have his headlights capture the embracing young couple? None other than the college's new president, Dr. Roe.

As you might imagine, at a Bible college in the 1940s public displays of affection were not allowed. Dr. Roe didn't confront them on the spot; he drove to his office and then summoned Georgina.

We're engaged!

"It's all right," Georgina proclaimed, "We're engaged! See, here's the engagement ring."

"Hmm," the new president narrowed his eyes as he pondered the dual violations of protocol (neither public displays of affection nor engagements were allowed among the students). "Who gave you permission to get engaged?" he asked.

"The Vice-President, Mr. Gillingham."

11

Dr. Roe pursed his lips as he pondered the situation. Then he nodded, apparently affirming his colleague's decision. "You may go, Miss DiValentino."

As it turned out, six couples at the school were serious about getting married. The school could change its policy on students not marrying, or it could risk losing up to twelve students. A huge state-run university wouldn't notice the loss of a dozen students, but a small Bible college couldn't afford to lose such a significant percentage of its student body. Besides, the college certainly saw marriage as a God-ordained and honorable institution. There really was no reason not to change the policy—so, following a special school board meeting, that's exactly what happened. The school even bought a building for married-student housing.

Navy Life

An impending marriage was no basis for excuse from military duty, even if his country had just prevailed in the biggest, costliest, and deadliest war the world had ever experienced. Upon graduation from Swarthmore in 1946, David, who had been enrolled in the Navy's V-12 Unit (similar to ROTC), was commissioned as an ensign and soon after had to ship out on the USS Cleveland, a light cruiser.

On March 16, 1946, about two weeks before the Cleveland left port, David wrote to his parents,

Ensign Solt was ready for life at sea.

Well, tomorrow is my birthday and so I'll be able to start reading your daily readings.

Now to get to the purpose of this letter, and that is to ask you for a specific wedding present, but I'll bet you can't guess what it is. Well, it's the car, and Georgina and I would like to use it on our honeymoon.

We now have set our wedding date for July 13th, and after this we want to go on a five-week honeymoon. We plan to set out for Niagara Falls and then over Lake Erie to Detroit. From there to Chicago, Mountain Lake, Yellowstone Park, then down through

12

Washington, Oregon, and California. We'll come back through Grand Canyon, and then Newton, Kansas.

But before marriage, duty aboard the CLEVELAND called. With the war over, David, a gunner, fired only at inanimate targets—imaginary enemies. On May 25, 1946, a Naval publication reported, "The high spot of ship life has been the execution of firing exercises. Latest figures indicate a good score for the CLEVELAND in preliminary practices. We had no injuries."

The Call to Missions

David had graduated from high school and enrolled at Swarthmore when he was just seventeen, and he graduated from Swarthmore not long after his twenty-first birthday. Then he enrolled at PSB, where he took Bible classes in the morning. He spent his afternoons getting practical instruction at the Radio Electronics Institute in Philadelphia, while Georgina worked at Eastman Kodak.

Of the many chapel speakers at PSB, one really connected with David and Georgina—Bill Thompson, Home Director of the Latin America Mission (LAM). The ministry needed an electrical engineer in Costa Rica. David and Georgina knew little about Latin America, and ministering there had never before even crossed their minds, but among all the students at PSB, David was the only one whose credentials truly fit the need. He knew that—as did all the other students.

David and Georgina had already been accepted for special missionary training at Moody Bible Institute, so leaving soon for Costa Rica without the training at Moody was a big decision. David's pastor was the secretary of the Mennonite Foreign Mission Board, and he wanted David to go to India to install electricity in a mission hospital. But LAM offered the young couple a chance to pioneer an exciting new ministry—Christian radio. At that time only one other Christian radio station, HCJB Radio, existed in the entire world. Christian radio offered a new technology—a whole new way to bring the gospel to the masses, unlike any method prior to it.

When Mr. Thompson officially offered the position to the newlyweds, they asked for some time to pray about their decision. He

13

gave them the night; he'd be back for their answer in the morning! After a night of prayer and discussion, they were ready for Mr. Thompson's return. "Yes," they said; they would answer the call and go to Costa Rica. They then had a mere three months to complete mountains of applications and other paperwork and prepare for their departure— provided the LAM board voted to accept them.

The answer wasn't long in coming: accepted. Time to start raising the necessary financial support. In August David wrote to his parents, "We received a great thrill this morning when in the mail we got a letter from Perma Zerfass and in it was a check for $188.46. She got her leave money from the U.S. government and promised the Lord a certain part of it and so it was an odd amount. We do thank the Lord for this and the money that is coming in for our ministry in Costa Rica."

David and Georgina raised the necessary support in just six months, so they would soon be departing for Costa Rica.

Mr. and Mrs. Solt

July 13, 1946

In the spring, prior to the wedding, Georgina wrote this note to David's parents: "I don't' know if I told you this before; I got my ring Saturday a week ago. I was so glad to get it. David probably told you all about it. About the wedding cake, I'll write home and see if she can get 35 pieces out of it. I must buy the bride and groom for the top though. About the favors—anything will suit me just so it looks nice; you judge, [perhaps] that silver cup with peanuts and a bride on the side. As to the long dresses, my sisters aren't wearing them … I know … it isn't that formal. Miss you all, Love, Georgina."

When the big day finally arrived, July 13, 1946, David's brother, Paul, served as best man, and Georgina's sister Gloria was the maid of honor. After a relatively short and simple ceremony all the attendees retreated to the DiValentino home for a big meal before the young couple departed for their honeymoon, which was considerably shorter and less elaborate than originally planned, because preparations for their call to the mission field beckoned. They could, however, view the entire situation from a different angle: they were about to go on an all-expenses-paid extended honeymoon to the tropics—in Costa Rica. Then, as an added bonus, they'd get to share the gospel with their Costa Rican neighbors.

Chapter Three

New Life; New Land

℘

My mother, Georgina, was born in 1923, the same year, coincidentally, that the International Conference of American States held its fifth annual conference, in Santiago, Chile, during which the conference members began planning the Pan-American Highway. In 1926, the year my father, David, was born, the Mexican government began to build a system of modern highways that would become a major part of the Pan-American Highway.

It seems that, in God's providence, He chose to correlate my parents' birth years with two important events in the development of the very long and often treacherous road our family would struggle across several decades later on our way to El Salvador. Looking back now, I'm not surprised. Remember what God said when He called the apostle Paul to minister for Him: "I will show him how much he must suffer for My name's sake" (Acts 9:16). While our trials wouldn't begin to match those Paul encountered, in time, David, Georgina, and we, their children, would learn that ministry for the Lord does involve some sacrifices.

But in 1947, when my father and mother first answered the call to missions work—and were accepted by the Latin American Mission board—rather than bounce along the Pan-American Highway, they would fly from Tampa to San Jose, Costa Rica. But first they had to drive more than 1,000 miles of East Coast highways from Allentown to Tampa. And along the way they passed through a wicked tropical storm.

Mom wrote,

> *Practically the whole mission staff (20) was there to meet us and they really gave us a warm welcome.... We drove to the Seminario Biblico (Bible Seminary) and had supper. After supper*

16

they showed us our rooms and they are darling. We have a private bath, bedroom with double bed, and also a private living room. There were three large bouquets of flowers, carnations, roses, and gladiolas.

But while David and Georgina flew to their new, far-away home, both sets of their parents, though happy for them and blessed by their choice to serve the Lord, were absorbing the empty feeling that always gnaws at parents who watch their children leave for destinations too distant for frequent visits. That just might be the most difficult part of being related to a missionary.

Getting Started

As I wrote earlier, LAM was a pioneer in Evangelical Christian radio ministry—only HCJB Radio preceded it. HCJB's "Voice of the Andes" aired its first program from Quito, Ecuador, on December 25, 1931. That was quite a faith launch, as, by one estimate, at the time probably no more than thirteen people in the reception area owned a radio capable of receiving the transmission.

Sixteen years later, as my parents prepared to help launch the first such program for LAM in Costa Rica, their potential audience was significantly larger. But plenty of preparatory work would be required before the startup. Construction of the building for the station and the recording studio wasn't complete. Dad managed the construction, as well as helping with the labor. The tower still had to be erected—which also was Dad's duty to oversee. He also personally cut the steel and assembled the tower, much like assembling a giant erector set. Meanwhile, he and Mom studied Spanish and became physically and socially acclimated to their new home.

The TIFC Evangelist magazine of October 1947 included a short article announcing my parents' arrival.

A warm welcome was extended to Mr. and Mrs. David C. Solt upon their arrival in San Jose on September 27. David, a graduate of Swarthmore College with the B.S. degree in Electrical Engineering, has also taken his diploma as a radio technician in the Radio Electronics Institute, and has secured his First Class Radio Telephone Operator's license. Both David and Georgina studied at

17

the Philadelphia School of the Bible. Their Christian character, training and musical gifts will give them, we are sure, a real ministry in the Radio work.

About a month after my parents' arrival in San Jose, a shipment of their supplies arrived, including beds, dishes, clothes, food, and two unassembled bicycles, which David promptly assembled. One was the bike that in a few months he would ride amid the whizzing bullets of battling soldiers and revolutionaries on his way to the post office.

Ministry Amid Revolution

On a screen of the history of world events, from creation to the present, a forty-day revolution in a small Central American country in 1948 wouldn't register a blip. But to those living in Costa Rica at the time— and especially to the 2,000 casualties of the revolution and their loved ones—the battle between government forces and the National Liberation Army was big news.

Ulate followers march through the streets of San Jose in 1948.

My parents had been residents of Costa Rica for about five months when the fighting erupted on March 12, 1948. Popular history says the revolution was a reaction to a stolen election, and there certainly is some truth to that version, but the story has deeper roots. It really began six year before that, when Jose Maria ("Don Pepe") Figueres Ferrer was exiled to Mexico for openly denouncing and opposing the government of President Rafael Angel Calderón.

Ever since his exile, Don Pepe, who had returned to Costa Rica in 1944, had been looking for the right opportunity to topple the government. In 1944, Teodoro Picado, considered by many to be a Calderon puppet, was elected president. In the 1948 election, Calderon sought to regain the presidency for himself. When the votes were counted, Calderon's opponent, Otilio Ulate, a newspaper publisher, appeared to have won the election by some 10,000 votes. But the day after the elections, a fire of suspicious origins destroyed many of the ballots. Calderon's cronies, who still held the majority in the legislative assembly, annulled the election. Don Pepe found the rationale he'd been looking for to start the revolution.

I'm grateful that the revolution ended a month or so before I arrived on the scene, at Clinica Biblica in San Jose, on June 15, 1948. My parents—still in their early twenties, trying to learn a new language and adapt to a new culture, trying to master a new career, and now with a new baby—really didn't need the added stress of enduring a prolonged civil war in their new homeland.

Sovereign God

I understand that world events don't cater to the whims or even the needs of individuals or families, but, at the same time, I also understand that the sovereign Creator of the universe is fully capable of arranging the events of our lives so that they mesh perfectly with His overall plan. I truly believe that He protected my parents, my siblings, and me, as we ministered for him in Latin America.

At the same time, I also understand that sometimes His sovereign plan requires greater sacrifices on our part. Many years later, in 1974, I learned this lesson firsthand when my son Matthew was stillborn while my husband and I were in missions work. My heart was broken, but I learned to offer God the sacrifice of praise for His omniscience. Only He knows how the loss of this precious baby furthered the purposes of His kingdom. I rejoice now with the assurance that one day, in the full manifestation of His kingdom, I will be reunited with Matthew.

My mother told me that when my dad, not normally given to emotional displays, learned of our loss of Matthew he cried.

Daily Life in Costa Rica

Even before the civil war, my parents had their hands full just coping with daily activities. In December 1947, when my mother was two months pregnant with me, they moved into the seminary annex, where they had to share a kitchen with another young missionary couple. That was before they had a refrigerator, so, as they'd had to do since their arrival in Costa Rica, they shopped for small amounts of food daily and had to finish what they bought because they had no way to preserve it. What a relief it was for them when their nine-cubic-foot Kelvinator refrigerator arrived a short time after their move to the annex.

1948: David and Georgina in Costa Rica

Food prices in San Jose were reasonable for the era—bread for fifteen cents a loaf, hamburger for twenty cents per pound and pork chops for forty cents per pound—so they were able to fill the tiny refrigerator (by today's standards) weekly and dramatically reduce the frequency of their shopping trips and make their lives somewhat easier.

I, on the other hand, began to cause trouble long before I was born: the hormones I'd added to Mom's system caused her "morning sickness" that stretched well beyond the morning hours. She said smells such as coffee, bananas, or papayas made her nauseous, and that was a real problem in a country that grew and exported massive amounts of each of those products. Not surprisingly, as she always did, she learned to cope and thrive there in the tropics.

Two weeks before Christmas 1947, Mom wrote, "We had another delightful experience this morning; we went visiting with another missionary, Bob Spencer. We gave out tracts as we walked along. David and I practiced, 'Le gustaria leer este folleto?' (*Would you like to read this pamphlet?*') We met a lady that was very interested in the tract so we asked if she had a Bible, and she did. We had a wonderful opportunity to tell them about the Lord. We will go back again." Life wasn't always easy for my parents, but they had no regrets about their decision to take the gospel to the people of Latin America.

Costa Rica's Spiritual Soil
Previously I wrote that my mother's birth year, 1923, coincided with the conference that began the planning of the Pan-American Highway. That year also marked the formation of Costa Rica's Reformist Party, the forerunner of the nation's Communist Party, which formed in 1931. But communism never became as forceful in Costa Rica as it did in many other Latin American nations.

20

Before the arrival of Roman Catholic missionaries in the sixteenth century, Latin American natives were animists. Catholic missionaries introduced a new worldview; a few of the natives accepted it voluntarily; many more were persuaded or coerced to accept it. Protestant denominations had a paltry presence in Costa Rica and other Central American countries even four centuries later, when my parents arrived there in 1947.

In the mid-1800s England established a coffee trade with Costa Rica that would develop into the nation's signature export and primary source of income. The nature of Costa Rican coffee farming was egalitarian by the standards of the time. Even small coffee farmers prospered. In that economic climate, anarchist agitators would have had a hard time finding a sympathetic audience in the tiny Central American country.

The establishment of banana plantations followed the success of the coffee market, but along a different model. They introduced a true plantation model, with wealthy landowners and distributors creating a new class of impoverished field laborers who would soon become ripe for communist agitators and a brand of theology that later would be tagged with the label *Liberation Theology* (the notion that God's justice demands the overthrow of "oppressive" regimes).

But the banana business in Costa Rica never rivaled the coffee industry there, so the little nation, with its long history of relative fairness and cooperation never became as susceptible to communism and Liberation Theology as did many of its Latin American neighbors.

But neither was Costa Rica a model of democracy, and it certainly wasn't a utopia. This was the political climate in which Rafael Ángel Calderón presented himself as the alternative to the not-well-established Communist Party in the 1940 election. Not surprisingly, Calderon won, and he soon instituted many reforms. He also re-instituted religious (Catholic) education in the nation's public schools.

So, seven years after Calderon's first election, and a year before the brief revolution, my parents arrived in a country that had flirted with communism, had an on-again off-again on-again relationship with Roman Catholicism and the forerunner of Liberation Theology, and still retained some elements of its animistic past—all stirred together perfunctorily in a syncretic soup. Few had heard the plain, simple gospel.

All that was about to change. The January 1948 issue of TIFC magazine announced the official opening of a new department at Latin American Mission:

The TIFC staff: Mom, front row, far left; Dad, back row, second from left

The staff meeting was adjourned, and Radio Station TIFC had officially become a new department of the Latin American Mission. That which one year before had consisted only of plans, orders for equipment, and some potential staff members, had now become an organization with its own well-equipped building, and its enthusiastic staff ready for action.

Chapter Four

Growing Ministry, Growing Family

cx

M om went into labor just before noon on June 15, 1948, but I was in no hurry to greet the world—I was already two weeks overdue. In those days, before the popularity of Lamaze and the notion that men should witness the birth of their children, it was common for fathers to pass the time in a waiting room—or even to go on about their routine and wait for a call telling them they had a new arrival.

So, while Mom labored in pain at La Clinica Biblica, Dad resumed his work at the radio station. He arrived back at the clinic at 10 P.M. only to find that his wife was still in labor, so he read a magazine in the waiting room. Finally, at 11:50 P.M., exactly twelve hours after Mom's labor began, I arrived. Dad wrote, *"Lois really looked a mess until we scrubbed her with soap and water. Then she looked pretty in the little blue nightie I brought her."*

I arrived in La Clinica Biblica just before midnight.

My parents mailed and hand delivered nearly 300 birth announcements—they must have been very happy to be parents. A few weeks later Mom wrote, *"We love her so much and have so much fun with her. Everyone says she is so cute and they just rave about her. But we don't say anything but give the honor and glory to our precious Lord."*

Mom and Dad were proud parents. I seemed happy.

On July 13 of that same year, on my parents' second anniversary, Mom wrote, *"We thanked the Lord for each other again and asked Him to make our love continue to grow. These have been two precious years together in the service of the Lord. We also thank the Lord that at the end of these two years we have little Lois Ann. We take her to special meetings and she is good."* (I was good because I'd found my thumb, and sucking it proved to be very comforting—so I'm told.)

Jack of All Trades—and Master of Many

Dad was just twenty-two years old at the time, but Mom wrote of his remarkable ability to fix almost anything, from small and large appliances to motor vehicles to cameras. Mom added, *"When Alice Church's Jeep broke down as she was coming in from the farm (20 miles away) she called David. Alice said, 'He's the only one who knows anything about this thing* [the Jeep]!'" Sure enough, two hours later, the Jeep was repaired and back on the (mostly dirt) roads. Similarly, when the son of LAM founder Kenneth Strachan's car broke down, *"David brought them another mission car. He fixed the Strachan's car and cleaned and simonized it like it was his own before he returned it to the Strachans."* Missionaries need to know God's Word, but it also really helps if they're multi-talented and diligent, as my parents were.

With several other missionaries from the States in that region, my parents rarely lacked for English speakers to converse and visit with. But their Spanish was improving by the day, so they were not limited to visiting with English speakers. In fact, Mom began teaching Trino and Flora Araya and a young local girl conversational English (for free) on Wednesday nights; it proved to be a great opportunity to witness to them about the Lord, and, sure enough, before long each of the three trusted Christ as their Savior. The Arayas and my parents remain friends sixty years later and still communicate from time to time in their retirement.

24

Because of my parents' many years of photography experience, thanks largely to great-grandpa Walp, they also did a lot of camera work for their fellow missionaries. Not surprisingly, then, in addition to all his work at the station, and his handyman work at home and for other missionaries and neighbors, Dad also found time to lead a photography club, which also proved to be a productive avenue for personal evangelism.

With the station up and running, they had plenty of evening hours of air time to fill. The hour-long 6:30 program "Favorite Hymns" consisted of best-loved hymns of the church interwoven with brief explanations pointing to the cross. At 7:30 they had fifteen minutes of Bible reading with the Hammond organ providing background. Then they ran "Heroes of the Christian Faith," a program written and narrated by one of the Costa Rican staff members.

Dad spent a lot of time at the station.

Each night they closed with "Evening Meditations," a program that aimed at getting people to make decisions for Christ. By July 1948 TIFC was broadcasting four hours a day, from 5 P.M. to 9 P.M.

Neighborhood Evangelism

On September 11 of that year, Mom wrote,

> We have been praying about buying a 1938 Buick and asked the Lord whether we should get it. The mission was advertising it in the paper for $850, but the field council met and on their own voted to offer it to us for about $600, and in addition they also voted to pay a monthly allowance if we use it to transport missionaries to and from the radio station. We feel the Lord has led us to buy it.

They had to be judicious about their driving, however, as gasoline in Costa Rica cost forty cents per gallon at the time (compared to about twenty-five cents per gallon in the States), and the Buick got just eight miles per gallon!

On September 22 my parents went out to visit some of the locals, along with Phil Smith, the acting station manager and David Araya. Mom wrote about that:

> Some of the homes were just like stables for cattle, and even worse. In one home occupied by a widower, there were no chairs to sit on. Another house had just one bench, and they offered their bed to sit on. Three in the family, and they had one bed that had a dirty cover. The son and mother in that family accepted Christ.

On a later visit they learned that the local priest had visited the family and scolded them for listening to the Protestant Christians, so the family members would not come out to talk to Phil and Dad.

On October 7, Mom wrote,

> We got back our written Spanish exams and we passed, praise the Lord. Now we are slaving away at the memory work. We are so tired and drained; we know not what to do. So we have planned a weekend at the orphanage in the mountains about twenty miles out of the city. Joe and Ruth Coughlin will come along.

Dad added this about the trip:

> We got stuck in the mud on the way to the Finca (farm and orphanage) because it was raining. Four men came along and helped push [the car] so we could drive on to the rest home. We had so much fun. Saturday we went horseback riding for three hours and I did not get sore, which is surprising since this was my first time on a horse.

A Much-Anticipated Visit

Dad wrote this note to his parents on October 17: "We bought your round-trip tickets for $187 each. This was a saving of about $50-$100 on each ticket. We are so excited that you will be coming on Dec 13th." I would soon meet my grandparents—though I was too young to understand.

By Thanksgiving of that year we'd moved into our new home, a six-room house just twenty-five feet from the new radio station. That move really aided my parents as they balanced their many duties at the station with caring for a baby. Dad was especially busy with the short-wave transmitter, and Mom, having taken on the role of station librarian had her hands full—when she wasn't caring for me—with sorting and cataloging records.

A few days after Thanksgiving, as we returned home from a trip into San Jose, the window on Dad's side of the Buick suddenly exploded. Dad's chin was cut as all of us were showered by tiny shards of glass. Thank God that was the only injury. Fortunately, the bullet hit the chrome window panel before glancing off and breaking the window. Had it come directly through the window, Mom might have been a widow with a new baby to raise.

Before long the Costa Rican police discovered that a worker at a nearby farm had sought revenge on an enemy who drove a car like ours. My father nearly paid the ultimate price for that man's case of mistaken identity. Dad sent his parents a note asking them to bring a replacement window for the Buick on their visit, which by then was just two weeks away.

On the big day of Grandpa and Grandma Solts' arrival, I suspect my parents were beside themselves with joyous anticipation—although I was much too young to remember their arrival or any of the visit. I'm sure Dad and Mom were similarly sad when the day arrived for Grandpa and Grandma to leave. But, again, that's just part of missionary life, and my parents understood it.

Life in Canas

Work at the station continued in a mostly routine fashion for the next few months. But on July 21, 1949, Mom and Dad learned that a new arrival would interrupt the Solt household by late autumn or early winter. They expected a boy, but that was long before the era of sonograms, so it was just a guess.

A short time later, my parents agreed to house-sit for the John Lenko family, missionaries in Canas (pronounced Can yas), who were returning to the States for furlough. Canas is northwest of San Jose, near the border with Nicaragua. Meanwhile, Joe and Ruth Coughlin, yet another missionary couple, came to fill in for Mom and Dad at the station. Missionaries need to be adaptable as well as dedicated and resourceful.

Mom wrote,

> *We took a train to Puntarenas and slept in a little rooming house and got up the next morning at 4 a.m. We had a grand plane ride, landing in pastures, with animals all around. The plane was all splattered with cow manure. We took the round about flight to see Liberia, Nicoya, and a few other small places, mostly mountainous. The Lenkos were at the pasture to meet us. Every place kept getting a little worse as first there were Jeeps to meet the plane, then it ended up oxen and horses which met the plane. Even the fire extinguisher was on the oxcart. How wonderful that the plane can get in where there are no roads.*

My parents were happy to help a fellow missionary family, but again, doing so meant some sacrifices for our family. First, because of the lower elevation, Canas is hotter than San Jose, and that was especially difficult for me, at the time a one-year-old baby who was learning to walk. And as any good parent knows, when your baby hurts physically, you hurt even more deeply emotionally. In addition, Mom and Dad had the added challenge of preparing meals in a locale where produce was hard to obtain, and in a house that lacked most modern appliances. But, typically, they soldiered on without complaining.

Dad had completed his construction of the 350-watt shortwave transmitter back at the TIFC station before we left for Canas, so my parents were able to listen and keep up with happenings back home. Mom wrote,

> *There is always someone coming in to talk, and we must be polite to them and sit and talk too. One fellow walked four hours each way just to get some books and tracts. Another fellow rode seven hours on horseback to come for medicine and to get tracts. Don Agapito comes hobbling on his cane to every service, whether it is raining or not. He came to know the Lord after being stricken with polio a few months ago. Since his eyes have been affected he comes several mornings a week so David can read the Bible to him. We write verses in large print and he sits in the park memorizing them.*
>
> *The buzzards come right into the yard; the roaches are all over the toilet seat, and at night they sort of tickle when you are sitting*

for any length of time. Lizards crawl here and there. We have no ice here in Canas, and the coldest water we have is what is in the earthen crock. We have a lot of work with people and teaching SS, church, young people, Tues Bible study, and Friday prayer meeting. We are all alone here except for the Lenko's maid.

Back to the Station

We returned to our home near the station in mid-September, and by then I was walking quite well. Mom wrote, *"Lois is here in the radio station with me and she just points and talks a long line of words. She is cute. She really walks all over but she doesn't molest things."*

By mid-October, the station was broadcasting daily, from three to eleven P.M. My parents were excited to learn that people were reporting receiving the broadcasts from most Central American countries, from Mexico, from many states in the U.S., and even from Canada.

My first sibling arrived December 10, 1949. Mom wrote,

> *Lillian Ruth has arrived. Saturday I wasn't feeling well and came to the doctor, who gave me a shot at 10:30 A.M. Lillian arrived at 1:30 P.M. She came so fast and the last half hour no one was ready for her, so I had her in the labor room. She weighed 7 lbs. 2 ounces, had long black hair and small eyes. I took a picture of her and so we'll send it soon. She is much darker than Lois and really ruddy.*

Eight days later, Mom added another note:

> *Lillian is the sweetest little bundle and we love her all the time. Lois just loves to hug her and kiss her. She comes into our bedroom in the morning and the first thing she says is "Chee, chee" (baby in Spanish).*

The tower parts arrived, but none of the local men had the experience required to assemble a radio tower, so the station employees would have to erect the 200-foot-tall tower. Dad ordered special shoes with cord rubber soles and a steel shank for climbing on the tower parts during the

Fortunately, Dad was never afraid of heights.

assembly process, but they still hadn't arrived by July. He assumed someone stole them en route. So he had to stand on the thin, hard metal tower sections wearing his thin-sole shoes, which, I learned later, was very uncomfortable.

Each section of the tower was ten feet long. In addition, they had to drill more than 100 holes into each section. They also had to use vinegar to remove the galvanizing from each section before painting it. All that *before* assembling the pieces! Then, when the assembly actually started and the tower began to grow, Dad was the one who had to climb up and actually do the assembling, along with a national. I suspect that if I'd been old enough to understand what my daddy was doing I'd probably have been quite afraid for his safety.

In May 1949, Mom wrote,

> *Lois (2 yrs.) and Lillian (5 mos.) are over here in the station with me. Lois sometimes sings at the top of her lungs! She is now pulling up Lillian's dress and patting her stomach. Lillian is just laughing and cooing at the top of her voice. She is so cute.*

A few months later, in November 1949, a survey discovered that of the twenty-five radio stations available in Costa Rica, TIFC was the fifth most popular.

Chapter Five

New Decade, End of an Era

CR

My parents were truly grateful for all the volunteer work Grandpa and Grandma Solt did for us and for the ministry. They filled orders for the station, did prayer letter mailings, and even monitored the quality of the signal reception. They also cared for I.R., who, as I mentioned earlier, had come to spend his final years with them. I.R. went home to his Savior in June 1950. For the Solt and DiValentino families, I.R.'s passing was the end of an era.

My parents really missed I.R., and I'm sure I would have too if I'd been older and had known him. They were especially grateful that I.R. had introduced Mom to Jesus and then introduced them to each other.

Promise of a Special Christmas Present

On July 8 Mom wrote another note to Dad's parents:

> *Lois and Lillian play so cute together. This morning Lois had some paper and Lillian did all she could to reach it so she could eat it. Lois did a good job of keeping it away. Honestly, Lois just loves her and kisses her, plus tormenting her, of course. But Lillian loves her company. I have begun to wean Lillian. We can hardly wait until you are here to enjoy them with us.*

Grandpa and Grandma had proposed another Costa Rica visit for October, but my parents suggested that it would be better to wait until around Christmas time so that they'd be able to meet the new present set to arrive three days before Christmas. Yes, another Solt baby was on the way.

Meanwhile, relations with the local Roman Catholic priest were less than genial. He was preaching against the station. He told those who

31

were listening to the programs that they needed to return to the Catholic Church and confess for turning from the "true church." So it came as no surprise to my parents when, in August, the neighbor who previously had allowed the new radio station employees to place the long-wave antenna in his tree now announced that he wanted to chop down the tree.

Earthquake!

Work on the tower continued through late summer and into autumn, but on October 5, everyone had to pause and reconsider the risks involved in erecting a 240-foot radio tower in an area prone to earthquakes. The following article from the LAM Evangelist magazine tells the story:

> It was a Wednesday morning in San Jose, Costa Rica. As missionary David Solt put on his safety belt and prepared to climb the half-finished tower of radio station TIFC, he had no idea that God's calendar for that day read, **"October 5, 1950-Severe earthquake in central Costa Rica."** But even had he known, he probably would have gone anyhow.

> For weeks Dave and his fellow missionary-engineer, Phil Smith, had been working at the laborious task of cutting and drilling steel for the home-made radio tower. of the Latin American Mission's new station. Base insulator, guy cable, guy insulators, steel and hardware were all on hand. And the first 50 feet of steel sections, weighing altogether half a ton, were up.

> Dave, who had elected the dangerous job of in-the-air construction for himself, was gambling his very life on that tower. He knew that during erection of one of HCJB's towers, two men had been badly injured and narrowly escaped death when it crashed to the ground. Fortunately, he did not know that one man was to be killed building the missionary radio tower in the Philippines and that two men would fall off during construction of TGNA's tower in Guatemala.

> The procedure Dave had to use on TIFC's new tower was daring. Up to a certain point, he could work with his safety belt on. But the tower was being assembled in ten-foot sections weighing some 200 pounds each. When the time came to fit each new section into place, Dave had to brace himself on the very top of the old

section-with no safety belt. Feet planted as securely as possible on the steel girders, he would lean down, head between his knees, to pull up the water pipe which served as boom for the new section. And even fearless ex-sailor Dave admitted that it made him dizzy!

Today, however, his job was somewhat different. Now that the tower was up to 50 feet, about one-fifth of its eventual height, Dave and Phil felt a sudden impulse to change their plans and put up a temporary set of guy-wires. The planks which were serving as supports looked, all at once, dangerously inadequate. And- so-up-he went:

It was early morning. Dave had already learned that to work after 10 a.m. was impossible because of the winds. But since earthquakes have no seasons and give no warnings, he did not know that nature was to send more than winds that day.

The same morning, farmer M. T. Gehman of Ottsville, PA., was working out in his fields when a frightening premonition came over him. He was a sensible sort of young man, not given to seeing visions and dreaming dreams. But for some reason the strange feeling persisted.

He could not shake it off. He and his wife, deeply interested in missions, often prayed for friends on the mission field, among them the David Solt family of Costa Rica. Never before had such an inexplicable panic taken hold of his heart. Finally he dropped his work and ran, as if driven by an unseen hand, into the house. "Where are you?" he shouted to his wife. "Come and pray with me. We must pray for David and Georgina. I fear they are in some terrible danger." It was obvious that he meant what he said. They dropped to their knees.

Shortly after, God's clock moved around to the appointed time for the earthquake in Costa Rica. Suddenly, the ground took a devastating lurch. Women and children in San Jose dashed screaming out of their houses, falling o n their knees and calling on the Virgin Mary for protection. Cement buildings swayed precariously. Dishes smashed to the floor. The shacks of the poor crumpled and crashed.

33

Out at the little farm on the edge of town where station TIFC is located, the 1,000-pound steel tower swung in a wide circle, back and forth. The new guy wires seemed to scream with the tension. And Georgina Solt's heart almost stopped, safety belt or not, surely Dave had been thrown from the tower and was broken and bleeding, perhaps dead ... but her husband was safe on the ground. Only a bare ten minutes earlier, he had finished tightening the last bolt on the tower, come down and ambled over to the doorway of the farmhouse that served as station headquarters. As the ground continued to quiver with that frightening uncertainty of all earthquakes, Dave stood safe, watching and praising God that he had finished putting up the guy wires in time to save the tower.

Not until recently, when he went home on furlough and gave a deputation message in the Gehman's church, did Dave learn the full story of his wonderful escape. Why hadn't they written, when they had received his letter about the earthquake and knew that the times coincided so perfectly? Well, after all, it had been God's doing, not theirs!

Back to Work

By mid-October the new antenna tower was more than half completed. But it was at about that time that Phil Smith decided that he should no longer climb up to work on the tower with Dad, so the station hired a local man named Antonio to help Dad finish the construction.

Building the tower was hard work. On a Sunday afternoon in October—although the tower was still under construction—TIFC staff held an official dedication ceremony.

A TIFC Magazine article from that time stated,

The fast-rising tower on the grounds of Radio Station TIFC on the outskirts of San Jose is an even more expressive symbol of God's great name. It is a vertical radiator, an antenna charged with radio frequency that will take to thousands of Costa Rican hearts the saving significance of God's redeeming love. More than other towers, this one stands for all that God means to us—it is dedicated to the service of the gospel and will radiate only those programs that proclaim, adorn and undergird the message of salvation.

Unfortunately, also at about that time, a heavy rainstorm began and work had to be halted briefly. The storm was so intense that airplane traffic also was halted because the runways had become mud pits.

Dad hoped the work stoppage would be brief, as a few earth tremors had shaken the area in recent days, and he and the crew hadn't finished attaching the stabilizing guy wires. For all they knew, another earthquake was imminent. But as they waited, Mom and Dad laughed as they watched their two-year-old Lois stumbling around the house while attempting to wear Daddy's work boots.

Elizabeth Mae

On December 6 and for several days following, everyone connected to the Latin American Mission mourned the death of Mrs. Harry Strachan who, along with Mr. Strachan, had been God's chosen vessel to pioneer the mission.

Almost as if to cheer the mourning LAM staff, on December 16, while Dad was at Puntarenas shore with Grandpa and Grandma Solt, Lillian, and me, back in San Jose, Mom's contractions began while she was Christmas shopping with her friend Edna Lionberger. Edna got Mom to La Clinica Biblica, and Elizabeth Mae arrived at 9:05 P.M. Dad was kind of disappointed; he really wanted a son this time. But adorable little Elizabeth quickly won him over.

The mission owned this Puntarenas rest home across the street from the ocean. It was a wooden house on stilts that rose out of the sand. We had to check our shoes for scorpions before we put them on. We could play under the house in the dark sand during the heat of the day. We played on the beach and in the ocean, wonderful times with some of our missionary friends. We called many of them "aunts and uncles." (The Stevens, Kinches, Burtons, Strachans, Roberts, Worsfolds, Gays, Smiths, Howards, Foulkes, Nelsons, Hoods, Longworths, Pretiz, Milre Lisso, Vivian Gay, Stumpfs, Miss Thor, Miss Neely and others that helped us in so many ways. They became our extended family far from our real family.) At night we would walk down the boardwalk or pier and buy Dos Pinos (pinyos) ice cream and just talk.

Another place we vacationed was called "El Descanso" (the Rest House) at Camp Roblealto, twenty miles away from San Jose, in the mountains. The farm was bought by founder, Susana Strachan, and had an orphanage for children from dysfunctional homes. The Christian camp gave kids and teens a lot of fun and Bible teaching several times a year. We missionaries used the Rest House, which had a beautiful view of green pastures and coffee fields for times of rest. It was a beautiful wooded area with a cooler climate that we all enjoyed.

So, meanwhile, in addition to all their work at the station, my parents had to care for two-year-old Lois, one-year-old Lillian, and newborn Elizabeth. We were a handful. Mom had to keep an especially close eye on her curious firstborn.

The Solt family had grown to five.

One day in 1951, when I was two-and-a-half, Mom suddenly realized I was nowhere in sight. The back door was open, so she went through and found no sign of me there. Close to panic, she ran to the front of the house that was close to a two-lane asphalt road. There she saw her little Lois, calmly walking down the middle of the road—with a bus directly behind me! Fortunately, the bus driver had seen me in time and was following slowly behind me, at my pace.

My parents dreamed of building their own home and were looking for land, but it was too expensive. They decided to ask the mission about building a house in the lower half of the finquita. Housing was a problem for the mission as it was growing in number. When my parents would leave Costa Rica the house would remain as mission property. Leon Headington helped measure out the foundation for the house.

Enrique Cabezas, a civil engineer, gave Dad some advice on the house. The plans for the house were passed by the field council, so work on the house is going forward. Dad had brought a block form from Pennsylvania to make all the concrete blocks for the house, but they made 58 of them and 10 cracked. There was a shortage of water to make blocks. So they made a small pool with cement blocks and filled it with

36

water so all we kids could swim! The Strachan, Roberts, and Solt kids all enjoyed it.

Discouragement and Loneliness

On March 22, Maritza, my parents' household helper, quit. Then a woman who was helping with the radio music cataloging quit. Then the Stumpfs, who were to help with music at the radio station, left for America. Mother and Dad were feeling very discouraged.

Then, on top of all that, Dad was about to leave for a two-week missions conference in El Salvador. For the first time since their wedding day, my parents would be apart for an extended period—and Mom would have to cope with three precocious babies all alone. If all that weren't enough, someone stole Mom's wallet while she was shopping. The trials might have been enough to send her into despair, but she saw the silver lining. She wrote, *"One thing that has encouraged me was that on Sunday I had 23 girls in my Sunday school class."*

At 11 A.M. on March 28, five Jeeps, overflowing with thirty-six people and baggage, left San Jose to attend the 100th anniversary celebration of the Central American Mission in El Salvador. The celebration and conference was to be held in the Mission Church in San Salvador from April 1-8.

Dad wrote,

> *The five Jeeps had trouble staying together, and because of the dust we decided to pass the others. As we neared San Ramon we had our first flat tire. The other four Jeeps arrived as we were mounting the spare tire. In checking out the other Jeeps we saw that two others had flats, so we were there a while. We were heading for Liberia, where we would stop for the night. When we got to Las Canyas we got gas and went down to the river to wash as there was no water in that town.*

> *We were told that it was dangerous to go alone to Liberia because of the bandits along the road, but we pressed on. At one point we thought we might be cut off by forest fires as they were burning right up to the edge of the road.*

> *After this we came to the first big river and the lights of the Jeep did not light up far enough across to show us where we had to*

cross. We heard that there were some holes as deep as fifteen feet. A man across the river started down the bank and waded through the river, showing us where to cross safely. Soon we came to another big river. It was dark and we could not see across, but two men appeared with flashlights and they pointed the way to cross. Praise God for His help. As we continued we were on bad roads with big bumps and rocks, which were hard to see at night. We arrived in Liberia at 9:30 P.M., more than ten hours after leaving San Jose.

The next morning we were ready to go on with only twenty-two kilometers to the Nicaraguan border. But it took about four hours to cross this distance. It is practically nothing but vertical inclines, up and down through the ravines where even a Jeep has trouble. The last ravine was filled with swampy water and logs laid lengthwise. The passengers walked and I tried to drive the Jeep across the slippery logs. After the border we had 150 kilometers to Managua, but it took quite a while because two of the Jeeps broke down. We crossed the border into Honduras, traveled three hours and reached the El Salvador border. Only 200 Kilometers to San Salvador—on paved roads! It took us thirty hours to drive 1,150 kilometers.

Their return trip was equally challenging, driving alternately through muddy marshes and a huge dust storm. Our family was joyfully reunited on April 12. But the joy was somewhat tempered by the continuing lack of water in our area as crews continued to work on the community's water lines.

Chapter Six

Life in Costa Rica—
and a Furlough

ↈ

Following Daddy's return and our resumption of a relative sense of routine, Mom and I accompanied Don and Jean Longworth with their little son David on a day trip to Puerto Limon to retrieve a package Jean's mother had sent her. The slow-moving train took eight hours to get from San Jose to Limon, and Mom later noted several colorful characters (some less than pleasant) that we encountered along the way.

Then, after the long, tiring train ride with fussy children, the Longworths discovered that, defying convention, this package had been shipped into San Jose. The long train ride had been for naught. Then, on the return trip we witnessed some tragic flood damage: a bridge had been washed out (not a bridge for our train), and a huge landslide (what appeared to be half an entire mountain), displacing many whose shanty homes were swept away.

House Construction and Routines

Meanwhile, Dad continued to work at the station and, when he wasn't working there, to make more blocks for the construction of our house. By early June they'd made some 2,500 blocks, about half of what they needed for the house. Meanwhile, since Maritza's departure, Mom had been unable to find reliable help for babysitting and housework, so she took a hiatus from her work at the station to be a full-time mom.

We girls certainly kept her busy. She wrote,

As I was making supper in the kitchen I put Lisbeth in the high chair and all of a sudden she was on the floor. She landed on her stomach and doesn't seem to have any bruises. She cried a little and then it was over. Lillian is another one who is always falling. Lois takes her to the bathroom to use the toilet and she is so nice about it. Lois says, "I'll take her, Mommy."

The other day I took Lisbeth to the bathroom and put her on the floor. She took off crawling, around the open door. She went for the kitchen. Does she go! I wish you could see her. She is so lively, just doesn't keep still for anything! She is certainly a wiggle worm.

On November 5 Mom noted that little Libet (Elizabeth) began walking. On that same day Mom recorded that Lillian began an agricultural enterprise; she planted beans, but rather than planting them in the ground, she planted them in her nose. Fortunately, they came out before sprouting, accompanied by many sneezes.

As Christmas approached, the structure of our new house was progressing quite well. Mom recorded that *"The roof beams are almost done on the house and the carpenters are ready to put the aluminum on it."* Meanwhile, much to the joy of his little girls, Daddy, for the second straight Christmas, set up an electric train set near the Christmas tree. He'd begun a new Solt family Christmas tradition.

While Christmas was a joyous season, it also was a busy season at the station for my parents.

Furlough on the Horizon

In mid January of the new year, my parents ordered the delivery of the new Chevy that would haul us on the long trip back from the States after furlough, planned to begin in August. The car would be delivered to Pennsylvania, where Uncle Paul would prepare it specifically for the needs of our family. For Dad and Mom, furlough meant returning home, but for my sisters and me, who had been born in Costa Rica and never known any other home, it would be an adventure to a new land.

Dear Uncle Paul and Aunt Myrtle Solt

But furlough was still more than half a year away. The Solt family still had plenty to do in Costa Rica. My Dad enjoyed adventure and welcomed any trip. So when Dean Lewis asked Dad to accompany him to southern Nicaragua to meet missionary Bob Remington, to help them drive their truck into Costa Rica, Dad eagerly agreed. My mother wanted him to go to the shore at Puntarenas with his family and the Longworths, but he asked, "How can I enjoy myself when there isn't any work to do there?"

So while Mother was enjoying the ocean breeze, Dad was stuck waiting in the south of Nicaragua: the Remingtons truck broke an axle in Guatemala. Meanwhile, Libet was with Thelma Nelson, so Mom was getting a real vacation. She was hoping that Dad would stop off in Puntarenas before he headed into San Jose. That didn't work out, and when Dad finally got back from the trip he was very tired; the doctor said he was just plain exhausted.

As construction work continued on the station and the house in Costa Rica, back in Pennsylvania, Dad's brother, Paul, was customizing the Chevy we'd use to drive back to Costa Rica from our furlough. My parents were always very grateful for all the work Dad's parents and brother did for them behind the scenes. Dad wrote, *"We appreciate so much what Paul is doing for us. Tell him so, will you. Maybe someday we can pay him back."*

The new house was taking shape.

By late March progress on the new house was such that my parents could begin to seriously contemplate living in it. It would be a while yet before it was ready for our family to occupy it, but it was taking shape. It would have four bedrooms, two bathrooms, a bedroom closet for developing photographs, a kitchen, laundry room, dining room, and a living room with hardwood floors. It even had a pretty, curved wooden staircase. There was also an attached garage and front porch.

Resistance and Response to the Gospel

On April 12, Mom wrote,

> This was a whole week of evangelistic meetings in the "Templo Biblico" church in San Jose, and souls are being saved. Tomorrow morning will be an early dawn service, and the Catholics are really trying to give us a hard time. There is a ball-park that has been rented so all the churches are participating in the early dawn service. The Catholics wrote a newspaper article saying that they owned the ball park and that it was not going to be rented for any Protestant service. Even though they are angry, the man who gave permission for the meetings stated that it was still on. There are no buses since it is Holy Week, so people are just walking. Well, Easter morning the park WAS NOT available!!! The Catholics announced on another station that there would be no meeting there. The service was then held in the basketball court in back of the seminary annex.

As our lives on Costa Rica went on, with the three little "Ls" (Lois, Lillian, and Libet) getting into mischief, Mom learned that her sister Gloria, who had attended Philadelphia School of the Bible with her, would soon be leaving to serve as a missionary nurse in Indonesia—we wouldn't be able to meet Aunt Gloria when we returned for furlough.

But despite the disappointment of learning they would miss Gloria upon their return, my parents were rejoicing, because that week more than 200 locals had come to know Jesus as their Savior during a week of evangelistic meetings. A week like that makes all the sacrifices worthwhile.

In Our New Home—Briefly

By late April little Libet was toddling around, biting the rest of us (Mom said she was teething), and we were ready to move into the new house where we'd have more room to escape the toothy little terror. By the beginning of May the move was complete.

Mom wrote that the move went well:

> It is just grand getting settled in this new house. We put up curtains and it looks homey and cozy. The house may not be painted right away

The "three Ls" enjoyed our new home.

since there may not be enough funds. They have also started working on remodeling our old home. The 3 L's are so excited about the tub! They have a grand time playing in the water. They also have fun playing "tag" as they run from the laundry room, into the living room, into the dining, kitchen and then laundry until they get weak from laughing or if one falls down.

On June 19, Mom took Libet to the hospital for her umbilical hernia operation, a typically safe and simple procedure. Mom wanted to watch the procedure, but the doctor said that Libet was so small Mom really wouldn't be able to see much. In those days, hospital stays typically were longer than they tend to be now. The doctors kept Libet there for five days, which Mom viewed as a reprieve from all the dust and noise that accompanied the building back home.

When Mom returned with Libet, she found that Dad had cleaned up all the sawdust on the floor, had hung the curtains, and had arranged the furniture. He'd even painted the master bedroom and hallway. With nearly forty guests in attendance for prayer, songs, food, and fun, the house was officially dedicated on July 9, 1952. But less than two weeks after moving in, it was time to leave.

Furlough

On July 21, 1952, we left for Panama, on the first leg of our journey to the States for furlough. While we were in Panama, Dad repaired the console at radio station HOXO. After a brief stay in Colombia, On August 9 we departed from Cartagena, bound for New York City by ship. We would remain in the States until March 1953.

We had a great time getting reacquainted with family members, and the Three Ls devoured the attention from grandparents and other family members.

Shortly after our return the local Allentown newspaper interviewed Dad for a feature article. The article gave readers a glimpse into the lives of a missionary family and recounted some of our more notable adventures, such as the bullet shattering the car window (the case of mistaken identity), which nearly made Mom a widow, as well as the close call with the swaying tower during the earthquake. The article concluded with a note about our busy furlough schedule:

The Solts will not have much of a vacation here, however, for they will be engaged in deputation work, that is, visiting churches throughout the nation and explaining their work to missionary societies and interested church groups. They hope to do this in every state in the union before they drive back to Costa Rica in a newly purchased small truck in April 1953.

Return to Costa Rica

Because of the need for deputation work, our time with family in Pennsylvania was shorter than we would have liked, but again, life as a missionary family requires sacrifices. By mid-March it was time to hit the road again. Inside the station wagon that Uncle Paul had customized specifically for our family was a bunk for me. On the bottom Libet and Lillian could sleep during the long hours of driving. In addition, Grandma Solt and friends made little gifts for us to open on the long trip.

We started out from Meyersdale, Pennsylvania, and headed west through West Virginia, Kentucky, and Tennessee, and spent the first night in a cabin on Kentucky Lake. The next day, as we drove through Arkansas and Oklahoma, we saw the damage done by a tornado that blew through shortly before our arrival there.

Snow had dusted the ground just before we arrived in Denver; and then, as we ascended into the Rockies, the snow became heavy. Dad had to stop and put the chains on the tires. We saw drifts that were as high as ten feet. But the weather cleared the next day, so we got to visit Rocky Mountain National Park. The following day, as we drove through Salt Lake City, we saw the Mormon Tabernacle. From there we went north, to Wyoming, hoping to see Yellowstone Park, but the snow was too deep; we couldn't get in.

As March came to a close, we passed through Portland, Oregon, on our way to the Pacific Coast Highway, where we'd turn south, toward California. In California we visited with Phil Smith's brother, Roland. We also saw Dayton and Grace Roberts, and then we slept at Nate and Marjorie Saint's house. (Nate is one of the MAF missionary pilots the Auca Indians killed in Ecuador.)

Later that week we traveled through a dust storm in the Mojave Desert, felt the earth rumble from a test atomic explosion as we drove through Nevada, and briefly visited the Grand Canyon, before reaching the border with Mexico to begin our first trip down the Pan-American Highway.

We savored our Orange Fantas.

After getting all the necessary paperwork completed for our trip, my parents filled our six-gallon water jug, filled the ice chest to keep the milk, and got each of the Three Ls an Orange Fanta soft drink. Then, as we passed slowly through Mexican towns, Mom and Dad let us girls toss gospel tracts to people who stood near the roads. Then traffic along the two-lane Macadam[1] road, where the speed limit was 120 kilometers per hour (77 mph), was sparse, so we made good time.

About 500 miles outside of Mexico City we met more traffic. Then we climbed to an elevation of 11,000 feet, to a section dominated by curvy, narrow roads. We traveled on, through Puebla in the mountains, down to Guatemala City. At another point the car had to be loaded onto a train for a twelve-hour trip by rail.

When we resumed driving, the roads were rocky and mountainous—often above 10,000 feet. Sometimes low gear could hardly get us around a curve. In addition, we had two flats within thirty minutes. When we arrived in Quetzaltenango we visited Naomi Gray, a classmate of my parents from PSB.

On April 21 we arrived in Honduras after traveling through El Salvador, where the roads were paved and generally in good shape. While in Honduras we visited radio station TGNA, and Dad gave a devotional to the staff. From Honduras we had a hard drive through Nicaragua on gravel roads. We met other people traveling from Costa Rica, and we shared with one another about the road conditions that we'd just experienced. My grandparents had written to my parents, and in

---

[1] Macadam was not the name of the road; it was a type of pre-pavement hard-surface road named after its inventor.

various towns along the way, including Managua, we were able to retrieve some mail.

Dad knew we'd have to ford some streams before arriving home, so in Nicaragua he bought four ten-foot-long wooden planks to drive over; two protruded from each of the two front windows. Fortunately, it didn't become necessary for them to roll up the windows because of rain before we got home.

River crossing were adventures.

When we arrived at the first stream, Mom waded across first and then Dad followed. They piled the larger rocks to the side, and then we drove across. When we reached the next stream, they spotted a big rock near the middle. The rock was too big to move; the car would get stuck if we tried to straddle it, so Dad hoped we could drive over it with one wheel. Unfortunately, the Chevy slipped off into the deepest part of the stream. We were stuck! The motor was out of the water, but the back end was flooded. It was good that the mattresses were placed up on the bunks and did not get wet, as many of our other belongings did.

Dad jacked the car up and put the boards under it, but after two hours still could not drive out. Dad was going to walk back to a town to find some oxen to pull us out. We'd been praying all along that the Lord would send help. Then, in answer to our prayers, four men came up on horseback and went for the oxen. We girls just played in the water and had a happy time while we waited.

The next morning, on the rocky road again, we hit a sharp rock, so Dad had Mom (at this point four months pregnant) sit on the hood of the car so she could spot large rocks and little pointed stumps that caused problems for the car. When we started down a steep

Mom sat on the hood of our new car, watching for rocks.

46

hill leading to a muddy gully we saw that our front wheels were pointing in opposite directions—the tie rod was broken. Dad left looking for oxen, but none were available. Fortunately, Dad was able to fix the rod himself. By the time he finished, it was late, so we camped on the side of a road, near La Cruz.

Chapter Seven

Back Home in Costa Rica

❦

On April 25, 1953, after traveling more than 3,300 miles across modern highways, through snowstorms, across scorching deserts, over twisting, treacherous, dirt roads in high mountains, and through several rocky streams, we were finally back home, in Costa Rica!

Sadly, soon after our return, robbers broke into our house by getting their arm through a small barred window in the laundry room and then unlatching the door. While we were all sleeping, they stole dishes, pans, candy bars, eggs, cheese, two electric irons, a sandwich toaster and clothes. It was quite alarming that even when Mom got up she heard

We enjoyed our new home, and so did the robbers.

nothing. But, apparently, when she flushed the toilet, they panicked and skedaddled. We praised the Lord for our safety. We little girls said that we were going to stay up all night and hit the robbers so they wouldn't come back again.

A twenty-crate shipment had arrived for us in Costa Rica just before we got back, so the entire family went to the port, hoping that the customs officials would be sympathetic and let us get the boxes out quickly. Instead, they spent four hours inspecting them and at the end charged us $600 in duty fees. We also had to pay $230 duty tax on the Chevy. Mom was ready to cry, but one of the missionaries told her it was normal procedure there.

Now is the Day of Salvation

Nate Saint visited us on his way to Ecuador.

On June 14, 1953, Nate Saint dropped by as he was flying to Ecuador. We visited for a while, and then Mom cut his hair before he resumed his flight. None of us knew what lay in his future, just two and a half years from then. In fact, none of us knows exactly when we'll die; that's why the apostle Paul wrote, "Behold, now is 'the acceptable time,' behold, now is 'the day of salvation" (2 Corinthians 6:2). And that's why my parents were so devoted to their Lord and the work He gave them to do. That's also why they were so happy that the Sunday school they'd started the year before in the Fenton's garage had grown to forty-three participants.

On August 2 of that year, Mom wrote,

"I wish you could hear the girls holler and yell. Sometimes I think I am going crazy when David teases them and it gets worse. I wish you could hear Libet talk, it isn't a quiet voice at all, but she comes out real loud and tries to get her idea across, and her eyes just about pop! David and I ask her to say it softer. She will for awhile, but then gets excited and starts off again real loud. You would really enjoy them now.

It's a Boy!

In September I started kindergarten as Dad and Mom continued their work at the station and as parents. On September 7, their parental workload increased by about twenty-five percent with the birth of the first boy in our little family. I'd hoped for a baby brother; Lillian wanted a girl; little Libet wanted puppies. Mom wrote,

At 4 A.M. they said, "It's a boy!" David and I were so happy and we thanked the Lord that it was a healthy baby. David seems to be floating on air as he has waited almost five and a half years for a boy. Now he thinks he's a man! David Lloyd weighed 7 ¾ pounds and he looks much like the others...a pug nose and fat cheeks. He's so cute. We have a very nice girl taking care of the 3 L's at home while I am in the hospital.

We celebrated Mom's birthday on November 12. She was thirty years old and she had a brood of four children age five and under to care for, plus a husband who worked very long hours, and still some responsibilities of her own for the station. Five days after her birthday Mom wrote,

> *I have so many people looking for a servant for me. Pray that I will get one soon since I have no one to leave the kids with when something happens to me, like spending the night in the clinic with amoebic dysentery and abdominal pain. They ruled out appendicitis.*

About a week later Mom could wait no longer, she had to go to the clinic. But with no one else to watch her children, Dad had to stay home and care for us, which meant Mom had to drive herself to the clinic, practically doubled over in pain and praying all the way. Turned out she had gall stones—painful, but not life-threatening, thank God. Fortunately, not long after that, my parents found a good nanny for us, her name was Anna.

A few weeks after the gall-stone attack, just as we were rejoicing over Mom's recovery, she bent over to pick something up off the floor and could not straighten up. Dad had to take her to the clinic lying down in the back of the Chevy. At the clinic the doctors gave her Novocain shots in the back, which provided temporary relief, but she struggled with back pain for the next five years, until she had surgery in 1958.

Eleven days into the new year, 1954, Mom wrote,

> *David Lloyd is such a darling. He now weighs 15 lbs. He just smiles all over himself and coos. He makes some funny noises when he laughs. The 3 L's just fall over him when he smiles at them. They like to crawl on top of him to hug him and kiss him better. They surely are monkeys to keep after.* Then she added, *Yesterday we had 54 in Sunday school and in our little tots class we had 30.*

A Wedding—and Ten Additions to Our Household

On February 2 Mom got a letter from her sister Gloria—she announced that she was engaged. Mom and Dad were happy for her, but surprised, they had no idea she'd met someone there in her missions ministry in Borneo, Indonesia. The man's name was Olav Nyheim; he was from Norway, and, like Aunt Gloria, he too was a missionary.

A few weeks after that we learned of a tragedy that had befallen a family from the Sunday school class my parents taught. The family shared a cheap apartment with five other families. When the roof of the poorly constructed building collapsed, a few of the people inside were injured. Our Sunday school friends were unharmed, but they'd lost their home. They had no place to stay, so my parents invited them to stay with us—all ten of them! Adding to the adventure, we had no electricity from 6 to 6:45 A.M., from 10 A.M. to noon and from 3:30 to 7 P.M., so Mom had to make all our meals ahead or cook on the Coleman gas stove.

In late March Mom wrote,

There is an epidemic of polio here now. They have eighty cases and seven of them have died. Most of them are pre-school age. So pray much for the health of all and that it might stop. A doctor came from the States to help fight it. Many people have been so frightened by polio that they don't send their kids to school. In one school they just had one kid show up. (One of the missionaries, Joe Coughlin, came down with a mild case of polio and could not move his arms. He was sent to the States.) By July 3 there were 800 cases reported with a 10% death rate.

Mom got pregnant again, but she miscarried on June 10. We were all sad for a while, but we trusted God's sovereignty. About that time Anna, the new nanny became increasingly sassy and troublesome. My parents tried to reason with her, and of course they prayed for her, but she continued to rebel, so they had to return her to her home. So again Mom had to care for four little ones with no help and while recovering from a miscarriage—and still dealing with her chronic back pain.

A Tragic Trip to Puntarenas

Our family needed a break, so we packed up and drove off for a short vacation at the beach in Puntarenas. We had fun playing in the water and on the sand there at the beach—but we'd pay for it.

First, as we waited at the train station in Puntarenas we witnessed a horrible tragedy. A young boy fell off a train onto the tracks and the wheels cut off his legs. The younger Solt kids must not have understood what had happened, but I did—I cried. The boy died about three hours later, probably from blood loss. When my parents learned of the boy's death they suspected that the authorities gave a halfhearted effort to save him because his family was too poor to pay for medical treatment.

Then, not long after returning home, we girls began to scratch our feet almost endlessly; the itch was almost unbearable. Mom took us to the clinic, and it turned out we had hookworms, almost certainly as a result of playing barefoot on the Puntarenas beach, where dogs are allowed to roam freely and leave their piles of worm-infested excrement. Hookworms can be very problematic. Fortunately, we suffered nothing more than the interminable itching.

It was at about that time that Mom had to deal with a problem from her oldest—six-year-old me. I loved potato chips, and when I learned I could buy small packages of them at school I started stealing money from Mom's purse. Then, to make matters worse, when she caught me with money that I had no business having and asked me where it came from, I lied and said Gracie Roberts gave it to me. It didn't take great detective work for Mom to discover that I'd committed the second sin to try to cover up the first one. After I got a much-deserved spanking, we prayed together for God to forgive me and to deliver me from the temptations. He did—both.

Dad's Solo Trip to the States

On October 1, Dad left for the States, to update many of our support churches on the progress at the mission and to get parts for the new 10K transmitter. Mom was sad at the thought of her best friend departing for nearly two months, and so were Lillian and I, as we were, by then, old enough to understand difficult concepts such as time. For a couple of little girls, ages five and six, two months seemed like a lifetime.

Grandpa and Grandma Solt meet David Lloyd.

A few days after Dad left, Mom wrote,

The children are real live wires! I sometimes wonder how I will hold up for two more months before David returns. Sometimes they are in a screaming mood and it drives me nuts. I gave them their allowance this morning. Thirty-five cents for Lois and 15 cents each for Libeth and Lillian. Five cents of each goes in Jesus' little African hut bank. They enjoy hearing their money plunk into the bank!

On November 22 Dad returned—he caught a plane from the port of Limon. Mom had planned to leave us kids with other missionary families and drive to Limon to meet Dad and bring him home. Instead, he arrived early with a suitcase full of fresh fruit and vegetables. It was a wonderful reunion—and just five days later Dad's parents arrived to meet David Lloyd for the first time. We Solt children danced with glee!

The Holts Come to Help the Solts

Dad really appreciated all the help from Mr. Holt, seen here.

On March 17, 1955, Horace Holt, a retired building contractor, and his wife arrived from Canada to spend some time helping Dad with his various projects. One of the first chores Dad and Mr. Holt tackled was building and then raising roof trusses for the new Nazareth church being built directly across the street from the radio station. Meanwhile, Margaret Holt helped Mom with secretarial and other duties at the station.

Meanwhile, David Lloyd was not only walking, he was running and, at times, was quite a handful—much like his sisters. But at times he could also be quite charming. Mom wrote, *"Lloyd is so sweet. I said the word clippers, and he came and sat on the chair while I cut his hair. He was so still and so good."* However, a few days later she wrote,

"He yells when you try to change his diaper. I give him slaps and then he hits me back. This morning he got into the sugar bowl, and I told him he was a bad boy and gave him some slaps. He got after me with one of the clothes hangers and kept hitting me. Who knows what he will be when he gets bigger."

Thank God, David Lloyd grew into a wonderfully kind man of God, but he did have a temper as a child—as we all did.

At about the same time that Mom was dealing with David Lloyd's temper, she had an even scarier episode involving Lillian and Lisbeth. Mom was over at the station when Lillian ran over to tell her that Lisbeth's head was bleeding. At the time she failed to mention the cause of the bleeding: she'd thrown a drinking glass at her little sister and it had cracked on Lisbeth's head, leaving a significant gash and a bloody sight that appeared to be even worse than it was.

Nazareth Church arches built by Dad.

In mid April the mission's field council decided to build another house on the finquita. Four college boys from the States wanted to go to the mission field; they'd heard about our work in Costa Rica, and they wanted to help. So the mission council decided that they could work on building the new house—under Dad's supervision. The boys, all big football players, would arrive in late June, after finishing their school year.

These four Wheaton College boys also helped with the construction of the Nazareth Church. They assisted Dad in building six laminated wood trusses, which were the first ever built in Costa Rica. These trusses weighed half a ton each, and they were raised with pulleys and help from Spanish language students in the area.

Nazareth Church was organized as a result my parents' Sunday afternoon visitations. They first met in the home of the Rodriguez family, with five children and their neighbors, the Bolandis, who also had five kids. Mother played the violin for the hymns and Dad led the service before he preached. Dad was the pastor for the first six years, before it was incorporated. The growing group moved into a missionary's larger garage. When they outgrew the garage they moved to the big studio at Radio Station TIFC. One of the members owned land across the street. He tried to sell it but the "For Sale" sign fell down three times and he felt the Lord leading him to give it to the group to build a permanent church building. The finished church was dedicated on April 17, 1960, with a full-time pastor, Rev. David Araya. Today the church has tripled in size to accommodate up to 700 people.

Chapter Eight

Para La Gloria De Dios

CR

On June 20, 1955, the four college students from the States—Chuck and Dick Geiser, Bruce Gale and Paul Groen—arrived to help build the new house. They stayed in our house (by this time the Costa Rican family who'd moved in after the roof collapse had long ago found a new place and moved out). Dad said they worked hard, and Mom said they were very nice and polite. The building project was going well.

The New Transmitter
On July 29 it was time to dedicate the new—and newly painted and functioning—10K transmitter. Mom and Dad sent out sixty invitations to the dedication. Mom wrote,

> We have asked the Lord for a day of no rain and the 29th was a beautiful day. The microphones, signs, and benches were put outside. Our hearts were full of happiness and praise to our heavenly Father for His marvelous provision. We put up a platform and a sign that said: "Para La Gloria De Dios, Mas Potencia, Mas horas, 6 am to ll pm." (For the Glory of God, more power and more hours). Monday we go on the air all day, which is a note of praise to God for all He has done.
>
> When the crowd came, Juan Isais said over the radio, "If you are listening by your radio you would be thrilled to see the crowd about 1,000 here in front of me." People were also given a tour of the station, and they saw the big blue ribbon on the transmitter.

Everyone was quite impressed and the event was interdenominational, which was nice. We had prizes for the best 50-word paragraph answering, "Why is TIFC my favorite station?" We gave three prizes. The man who won first place was from Cartago. Friends came to congratulate him on winning the Bible. He was not a believer but he still liked TIFC. Many unbelievers listen to the radio station, praise God!

Sadly, the local Catholic Church again saw this as an intrusion and as an affront to them, so they resumed their verbal attacks on the Protestants in general and TIFC specifically.

As summer wound to a close, the high school boys had to return to the States. They'd made good progress on the house. Meanwhile, the churn of nanny / house helpers continued, from Anna to Marta to Noemi, as life went on with its routine changes. Another big change was on the way: television, which had been available in the States for some twenty years, was going global. So Dad enrolled in a radio engineering and TV correspondence course from Washington DC. When TIFC added TV to its mix, Dad would be ready.

Personnel Additions at TIFC

In early September Franklin Cabezas, a Costa Rican, was named station manager, to start October 1. Costa Rican law required that the station manager be a Costa Rican citizen. The other TIFC staff members were happy to have found someone as gifted and competent as Mr. Cabezas. In addition, Irene Hungerpiller joined the station as a secretary. Mom was especially happy about that addition, because it would allow her more time for home visitations, which meant opportunities for personal evangelism. Unfortunately, not long after that her chronic back pain intensified. For a while she couldn't even stand.

In early November Dad got word that he should be able to get his Master's degree after one year of study when we return home on furlough. It hardly seemed possible that another furlough to the States was near enough to begin planning for it. A few weeks later, while Dad was in Guatemala for a radio and TV conference the 49-meter shortwave transmitter caught fire, so he had to rebuild it. He also was building a one-kilowatt ham transmitter so that they could talk to the States. Dad told his parents how to locate another ham transmitter operator in Allentown. With that accomplished, we were able to talk to Grandpa and Grandma Solt on a regular basis.

The Field Council voted to send our family to Panama from May to August 1956 so that Dad could fill in for radio station HOXO's engineer, who would be going on furlough. Then, after he returned to HOXO, we could start our furlough, and Bob Bedard an engineer from language school from TEAM would take over for Dad at TIFC. Missionaries often cooperate like that.

Martyrs

In highly developed nations in the post-World War II boom years, cars were becoming a necessity rather than a luxury. And those cars were not fuel efficient. More thirsty cars meant a dramatically increased market for oil that could be refined into the elixir that powered those vehicles. Not surprisingly, oil companies were always looking for new wells to tap. They found some promising sites in the Ecuadorian jungles—home to some of the most primitive people groups on the planet.

Tapping into those wells meant, again not surprisingly, encroaching onto lands those native tribes had historically claimed as their own. Nor was it a surprise that the tribes resented the encroachment. A confrontation seemed unavoidable. The natives, wielding spears and rocks would be no match for well-armed mercenaries hired by the oil companies (if the companies chose to go that route).

Well aware of the potential for a violent outbreak—and perhaps the loss of many natives who had never, ever, heard the gospel—our family's good friend Nate Saint, along with four of his friends, all of them relatively young, decided they had to reach the tribes people with the gospel before it was too late.

In late 1955, Nate flew his friends, Jim Elliot, Ed McCully, Pete Fleming, and Roger Youderian, into the Ecuadoran jungle, and together the five young men began to make gradual and guarded attempts to contact the Auca people. By this point they no doubt knew that the Quechua word *Auca* means *savages*—this mission would be no picnic.

But on January 5, 1956, three days after making camp on what the young missionaries dubbed "Palm Beach," waiting for their first face-to-face encounter with the Aucas, a picnic seemed to be exactly what was on the agenda. Nate's son Steve later wrote,

After three days of waiting on the beach, the men suddenly saw two naked women step out of the jungle onto the opposite bank. Two missionaries waded out into the river to greet them. When it was apparent the women were being well received, a man joined them on the beach. Dad's journal records that the three Huaorani seemed relaxed and acted in a friendly manner. They shared the missionaries' hamburgers and Koolaid and carried on an animated conversation as if their every word were understood.[2]

First contact seemed to be going well. But things aren't always what they seem to be. On January 6, Dad was at his ham radio when Phil Saint, Nate's brother called via the radio and asked Dad to try to contact Nate. (We were much closer to Ecuador than Phil was.) Nate's family hadn't heard from him and they were worried that he might have crashed his plane. Dad got no response either. Six days later, January 12, we got word of the massacre. All five missionaries were killed. It appeared that they didn't attempt to defend themselves.

On January 17, Mom wrote,

Our hearts continue to be saddened over those five missionaries massacred in Ecuador. HCJB had a memorial service in the air for them. They said the US Air force flew the five wives over the spot and dropped down a wreath as the plane kept circling until they finished their service in the air. David Howard's twin sister lost her husband, Jim Elliott, there. One was a close friend of ours, Nate Saint, the pilot. David Howard flew down to Ecuador to be with his sister, Elizabeth Elliot, and help wherever he can. Most of the wives plan to stay on. Aren't they brave? The Auca Indians were very subtle in trying to show that they were friendly when they were just laying a trap. I'm glad our Lord rules and what He does is right and we must just trust in His leading.

---

[2] Steve Saint, "Did They Have to Die?" Christianity Today, http://www.atanycost.org/images/DidTheyHaveToDie.pdf.

Just a few days after learning of the massacre in Ecuador, my parents got word of the death of a fellow LAM missionary in Costa Rica. Les Burton was at the Costa Rican border waiting for customs to open on January 16. At 1 P.M. Toddy (Les's fourteen-year-old stepson) and Les went to the river for a swim. As soon as Les walked into the water a shark took two bites out of his right leg. He swam for the beach and fainted. Toddy had to pull him out to the river's edge. Toddy ran up the hill to the customs house and called the men. When they got back to the shore, Les was dead. He'd bled to death. Dad later saw the right leg with a big bite behind the knee and a smaller bite in the calf; he said it made him sick. Via ham radio, we got through to Les's brother in Michigan and gave him the sad news.

Mom wrote,

Les' wife, Helen, is taking it hard as is Velma, Les' twin sister. They had the funeral this afternoon and the Templo Biblico was full. This is indeed a tragedy because Helen had polio when she was a child, so she can't bend one of her legs and walks with a limp. She has three children. Her first husband died suddenly of a heart attack. Helen looks as though she has aged ten years in this one week.

As a result of Les's death some boys up at camp Roblealto have accepted the Lord. Pray much that souls will be saved as a result of this tragedy. Missionaries have been deeply stirred by the Lord's taking six of his choice young men Home to be with Him. He never makes a mistake. David relayed this news to the Burton family in Michigan and the five missionary deaths to Philadelphia by ham radio because Philadelphia could not connect with Quito.

Another Furlough
A few weeks later, before my parents really had time to deal emotionally with the loss of their fellow missionaries, Bob and Juanita Bedards arrived. Mr. Bedards would be the engineer at TIFC and his wife would work as a nurse at the clinic while we are on furlough. Yes, another furlough was approaching and over the next eight weeks or so my parents had to prepare for it. Meanwhile, their lives as missionaries continued as usual, with the trickle of decisions for Christ beginning to build, gradually.

In addition, before we left, LAM opened its new Spanish-language Christian elementary school. Mom wrote,

> *LAM Spanish Christian school, Monterrey, is beginning to be a reality. School begins next week and it is beautiful. They have eight classrooms that are really modern. They have the electricity all hooked up and this was done in two days.*

Panama

Before the furlough in the States began we had to spend some transition time in Panama. On April 23, Mom and Dad borrowed a car and went around town looking for furniture, a stove and a refrigerator. The Mission gave them permission to use $500 for all of this. We stayed in our temporary house in the Canal Zone until June 15, when we found a nicer house to rent.

Meanwhile, Dad worked at the HOXO radio station again. However he had to take a brief break for an emergency appendectomy.

On the first day of August a huge storm rolled in and dropped so much rain that a good portion of our front yard caved in—it became a sink hole. We got through another trying situation; furlough was less than two weeks away—at least for most of us. Mom and we kids were set to leave on the thirteenth. Mom was eager to get home to her family because her dad had died recently. Dad had more work to do, so he'd leave twelve days later.

Chapter Nine

Furlough and Back

☙

D ad made it to Meyersdale in early September, in time to join us for the DiValentino family reunion, and just before he began his advanced studies in television programming at Temple University.

We had a marvelous DiValentino family reunion in Meyersdale during the 1956 furlough.

This was to be a longer furlough, so near the end of spring in 1957 my parents bought a twenty-seven-foot trailer and parked it on land owned by family friends, the Rice family, near their home and also near the home of the Gif Hartwell family. The Rices also had plenty of children, so we Solt kids had a grand summer playing with friends. Mom wrote of that time, *"Our hearts are full of praise to our precious heavenly Father who has once again supplied over and above what we asked or even thought."*

Dad was working with Gif Hartwell in collecting TV equipment and cameras for Costa Rica, but ultimately the LAM board rejected the idea of TV programming for Costa Rica. So all the equipment was then shipped to HCJB in Quito, Ecuador.

Not long after we arrived at our temporary trailer home Lizbeth fell from a tree and injured her hip, and it just kept getting worse until she was hospitalized in Syracuse Children's Hospital. She was diagnosed with osteomeylitis in her hip. She was seven years old and had her leg in traction. They tapped her hip and took out pus and injected penicillin several times. Her fever soared to 105 degrees, so my parents called the elders of North Syracuse Baptist Church to come and pray over her with anointing oil. After prayer her fever started to come down. She was very ill. There were four other children in the ward with her so she had good company.

By the time Independence Day arrived, Lizbeth was improving but not yet able to return home, plus Dad had a broken leg. A few days later a near hurricane-force storm hit; our little trailer nearly blew away. God never promised us an easy life. That seemed to be especially true for little Lizbeth. Her injury took a turn for the worse

Lizbeth was in her full-leg cast.

and the doctors put her in a full body cast—and this was at the height of summer. For such a little girl, she took it pretty well, but it was also no surprise that at times she became irritable.

That summer, Lillian, Dad, and I were baptized by immersion at Bethany Fellowship Church (one of our support churches) in Hatfield, Pennsylvania. Dad had been sprinkled as a child, but never immersed.

Back to Costa Rica Again

Eventually Lizbeth recovered, and on September 8, after Dad finished the summer semester, we left Allentown and began the long drive back to Costa Rica, with the trailer.

We hauled our "second home" back to Costa Rica.

Unlike the previous return drive to Costa Rica, when we first drove west and saw much of the States, this time, although we did stop several times along the way, we just went directly southwest, toward Mexico, where we could cross into Latin America. We made that crossing during the evening of September 16.

We drove on to Monterey, where we stopped so Dad could talk to the program director at the local TV station. We didn't want to leave the station and climb back into the stiflingly hot car, but we had to move on. Very soon after that we hit a stiff headwind that kept our speed at a maximum of about 35 MPH. We kids did get a bit cranky.

After a restless night trying to sleep at a busy truck stop, we continued to travel through mountains and then deserts that were hot and dry. We saw many Indians in their beautiful colored dresses, living in mud brick homes—with no roofs.

Mexico City was large and beautiful. We saw the results of a recent strong earthquake. Many buildings looked fine on the outside, but on the inside the walls were heaps of twisted reinforcing iron, broken bricks, and cement.

The streets were narrow, and at one place our trailer wheel went over the curb and as a result we had a broken axle one hour out of Mexico City. We had just started to climb the steep mountain and had to park on a curve. Dad took off the axle and went to have it welded. The

We "piggybacked" on a flatcar!

rest of us sat on the mountain for a day and a night, with parking lights and oil torches lit to keep us safe. We praised the Lord for protecting us in this dangerous location. Mom even had time to bake a cake, which brought some joy in the midst of discouragement.

With the Houks

As we drove through Mexico we noticed a car that had a sticker for Toccoa Falls, Georgia, on the bumper and thought it must belong to missionaries. Sure enough, it was Jim and Virginia Houk, with their three children, heading for Managua, Nicaragua.

One part of our travel included a train ride. Our Carryall and trailer fit on one flatcar, and our friends, the Houks, were on the next flat car so that we could eat together during the thirteen-hour trip. Our flatcar frequently became uncoupled from the rest of the train. What a trip!

In Guatemala we wanted to drive the coastal route, but one of the bridges was washed out, so we had to take the mountainous way, which meant climbing to 9,000 feet. It took almost an entire day to cross the steep mountain because we had to traverse a dirt road with hairpin turns.

We enjoyed travelling over El Salvador's paved roads, but every time we stopped we had an audience. The people had never seen a house trailer. The Customs officer stated, "It is a complete little house!"

Honduras had no roads at all; they were still in the process of building their state highway. We drove through plenty of mud and got stuck on one hill for ninety minutes. The fifth river we faced was the biggest and deepest yet. It was dark when we arrived, so Dad used a flashlight to investigate. He thought we could get

"It's a complete little house!"

through, but it was too deep and we got stuck in the deepest part. We prayed, and at 2:30 A.M. our friend Jim Houk arrived and pulled us out using his panel truck's dual traction. Not too much water entered the trailer, and praise God the engine started up again.

Back in Costa Rica!

Nicaragua had gravel roads except near Managua, which had paved roads, and that was where we said goodbye to the Houks. Soon after that we crossed into Costa Rica and arrived home on October 2. What a thrill it was to once again be on Costa Rican soil. We all sang, "Thank You

Lord for All You've Done." (My mother wrote, *"Someday we will write a book and include all or our experiences!"* Indeed...)

We were back home, and back in the swing of things, and for that, we were happy. But routine didn't necessarily mean peace. On November 1 Franklin Cabezas, my parents' dear friend and the manager of the TIFC station wrote the following:

In Latin America, unfortunately, the gospel has to struggle against a great barrier of prejudice. We Protestants have been portrayed for centuries as monstrous heretics, from whom it is necessary to flee at all costs. But, thanks to God, through radio we have a strong arm against the prejudices, so that now we are heard in homes where the door would be slammed in the face of a Protestant missionary. With the valuable help of classical music programs we are causing people to know who we really are and the blessed message that we preach.

To close out 1957, Dad managed to procure two turkeys, so we had guests; my parents prepared a Christmas meal for fifteen. But shortly after that wonderful event Dad had to go to Managua to start the ground work for the new radio station there. Mom was eight and a half months pregnant, so she wasn't thrilled about the timing of his trip, but it was necessary, so she coped. Vivian Gay came to stay with us.

Mark Charles Arrives ...

On January 10, 1958, Mom wrote this in a letter to our prayer and support partners:

*Mark Charles was born on January 5, at 8:45 P.M., and weighed 8 pounds, 4 ounces. He looks just like his Daddy. The "L's" were very excited about bringing him home. They all wanted a chance to hold him or kiss him. Lloyd shares his room with Mark and last night he said, "I'm sleeping with Mark 'cause I can call you, Mommy, when he cries and then help you take care of him because he's **my** brother."*

Mom added this in her letter:

One of our members lost her husband a short time before we got back in October, and her family practically disowned her for being an evangelical. They appropriated her furniture, and even went as

65

far as 'using her own bed and making her sleep on the floor on a mattress: She was very' much upset because. She had no other place she could call her own. Therefore, we helped financially, and carpenters lent a hand, and in one day we had a little house built for her on her own lot. It's nothing fancy, but she is very happy to have her own home.

... and Billy Graham is Coming

With Billy Graham set to come to San Jose for an evangelistic campaign in two weeks, my parents joined a group of evangelicals from many churches who closed out January with an all-night prayer vigil. The event was set to be held in the San Cayetano baseball stadium. Until then, Mom was busy taking care of baby Mark, who was still nursing, plus she was teaching women how to lead a person to the Lord, helping counselors get their papers together, and attending the counselor meetings. Dad was busy with committee meetings and the radio station. We were never bored.

Mr. Graham was to come in at the big international airport, and since it was so far out they made the official welcome for him there at the airport. Most churches cancelled Sunday school because everyone was to be at the airport at 10 A.M. Dad and Horace went out early to get the mikes and public address systems up so that everyone

Billy Graham came to Costa Rica in 1958.

could hear the interview with Billy and so that it could be broadcast over TIFC. The airport was packed.

The Catholic Church archbishop had bought ads in the newspaper admonishing people not to go to the meetings—saying that to do so would be a mortal sin—but even so, 10,000 attended. First, an evangelist from Puerto Rico spoke in the pre-campaign meetings. In these four meetings there were 125 decisions for Christ. Then, Sunday night, Billy Graham's preaching led to about 350 decisions. It was a time for Christians in San Jose to rejoice.

A Shocking Birthday Surprise

To celebrate Dad's thirty-second birthday, the Holts took my parents out for dinner at the Bal Moral, in downtown San Jose. Horace Holt was not only a great contractor and carpenter, helping around the radio station and orphanage, but he also had an impish sense of humor. Horace had hooked up a live wire to Dad's chair and periodically pressed the button, causing Dad to jump as though a bee had stung him. But that wasn't enough; Horace made sure that the waiter gave Dad a special glass that had several pin-sized holes that dribbled water on the front of Dad's shirt. It seems that everyone—even Dad—got a good laugh out of it.

Progress in Managua

Mom's back and hip pains were getting worse again, but the ministry had to continue, so in April Dad made another trip to Managua. The proposed radio station had been denied a frequency because the Catholic archbishop used his influence with Nicaraguan President Somoza to stop it. Dad and the other men prayed, then one of the men on the committee—who happened to be the vice minister of war—went to the president as a friend and convinced him to recant his earlier decision.

The station would be called YNOL, Ondas de Luz (Waves of Light), and the frequency would be 825 kilocycles. Dad was put in charge of the station. Our family began planning for our eventual move to Managua. But Dad would have more than just the responsibility for the new Managua station; on June 13, 1958, he was named Director of the Communications Division of Latin America Mission and was given the command of HOXO, TIFC and YNOL.

Later that summer we—especially Dad—had more adventures at the beach. First, Dad rescued two teenage brothers who had ventured too far out and were drowning. A short time later, we were at the beach again, and Dad was out bodysurfing on a wave when he saw a big shark nearby. Soon he and everyone else saw many sharks nearby—some even jumped out of the water. Everyone quickly came ashore and left the water to the sharks.

My parents wrote the following in their 1958 end-of-the-year newsletter:

We had hoped to say YNOL would soon be on the air, but as yet the land is still the delaying factor. The corporation has been formed, so this opened the way for the importation of equipment, the construction of the building and the erection of the tower. As we wait on Him, we know we will see Him do great things through YNOL in Managua.

We have purchased time on a local station at the shore Puntarenas. It is beginning to show results. People wrote in for free New Testaments and "Light of Life" course. Praise the Lord that Billy Graham's radio program, The Hour of Decision, will be coordinated and produced in Spanish here at TIFC and will be broadcast the first Sunday in January. Many stations throughout Latin America signed contracts to carry this program.

Chapter Ten

Managua

CR

D ad was supposed to return to the States in the spring of 1959, but, due to our temporary reassignment to Managua, the trip was canceled. In the April 1959 prayer letter, Mom wrote,

> *This is only a temporary assignment of a year or two until the station is operating smoothly by the national brethren themselves. We are thrilled and encouraged by the enthusiasm of these who want to reach the lost with the message of salvation.*

Our home in Nicaragua, supplied by YNOL, was on an eight-acre level piece of land about six miles out of the center of Managua. It was a

Our house in Managua was not luxurious.

typical Nicaraguan home, with three tiny windows, but five huge doors into the two rooms, and that didn't include the front and back doors. There were no closets or lights, no running water, and no inside bathroom. Dad had a lot of work to do. First he got us hooked up to running water—what a relief. But still it was far from being a paradise. Mom wrote,

> *There is a very strong wind this time of the year; and since it's very dry, the dust comes in between every crack and tile of the roof. We put up muslin curtains to keep out the strong sun rays as well as the dust, but it feels like a hot tent, so I don't know which is worse, dust on the food or the heat.*

Ants were a real menace, often turning entire sections of walls black as they marched their way, by what seemed the millions, through the abode over which they and we contested. Red clay tile covered the roof, and in the early morning sunshine, the big iguanas (lizards) lay out on top, enjoying the warmth of the sun.

The tiles were not cemented in place, therefore the many earthquakes or tremors jiggled them out of place. On a moonlit night, while lying in bed, we could see the moon and the bright stars. The clay tiles were re-laid before the rainy season began, but even so, strong storms often soaked much of the inside of the house. We were grateful that our time in Managua would be limited.

To start, the station broadcast for just two hours per day, from 6 P.M. to 8 P.M. Initially, the station's antenna was just a wire strung between a high tree and a high stepladder, so reception was limited—even within Managua. Dad ordered the materials to erect a 300-foot antenna tower. More climbing and dangerous work lay ahead for him and the men who would help him in the assembly.

The station started with a 500-watt transmitter, but Dad knew he needed something more powerful, so he planned to get a 10- or 15-kilowatt transmitter. At the time, I had little interest or understanding of such things, but I was happy Dad could do all these things.

Measles and Back Surgery

Not long after our arrival in Managua, we children broke out in rashes. At first Mom and Dad thought the rashes were merely a result of the heat, but then they worsened. Soon a doctor confirmed that we had German measles. We recovered, but we pouted some as the heat exacerbated the measles symptoms.

To make matters more trying, the previous occupants of the house had been less than fastidious housekeepers, so Mom worked hard to clean it, often spending hours scrubbing the filthy walls. That hard work aggravated her already fragile back, so much so that it soon became apparent that she would need to return to Costa Rica for surgery on two ruptured discs in her back.

We learned that the brother of Costa Rica's President, Dr. Oriomuno, was a qualified orthopedic surgeon who had the necessary experience for such a surgery. LAM president Kenneth Strachan was in Managua, visiting and observing the start of the new station, and about to return to Costa Rica, so he accompanied Mom for the surgery, while Dad stayed to care for us and to continue his work.

The surgery went well and achieved its purpose. Later Mom wrote, *"God's word sustained me (Isa. 30:15c). 'In quietness and confidence [trust] shall be your strength.'"*

On July 3, I wrote this to Mom, as we children attended the American school with diplomats' children:

We miss you very much. Tomorrow we are going to Lake Jiloa for a 4th of July picnic with missionaries. Yesterday we got our report cards and we were excited to see what our marks were. It is the teacher's birthday on July 17th, so I took a gift to her today: two hankies and one comb. Our vegetable garden is growing: we ate some radishes for lunch and the corn is getting big and so are the carrots. Yesterday we had no electricity or water. Daddy went down to the Jones for water, and we used the little gas stove for dinner.

Mom returned to us on July 14, and we kids were really excited to see her again, but Dad was especially happy. It seemed that each time they had to be separated—whether for a work assignment or for surgery—upon their reunion they realized a bit more how grateful they were that God had joined them together.

Another Revolution

A little more than a decade after my parents personally witnessed the Costa Rican revolution, our family found itself in the midst of another potential uprising. Communists had overthrown the Cuban government,

Nicaraguan soldiers guarded the station.

and tensions were rising throughout many Latin American countries, including Nicaragua. Consequently, the government stationed soldiers to guard LAM's YNOL radio station.

Despite the armed guards, a man who said he was a Christian and who had been hired as an on-air announcer stole several items from the station. The Nicaraguan police seemed to have little to no interest in solving the crime, so Dad hired a private investigator. The investigator obtained an arrest warrant, so Jim Houk and Paco Dona accompanied him to the city of Leon and found the man in a restaurant. He put up a fight, so they had to take him by force. We soon learned that we weren't his only robbery victims, but because of the lax criminal justice system, he was soon back out on the streets, no doubt returning to his criminal ways.

The Managua Radio Tower

The driver of the truck that hauled the tower sections to Managua refused to go any farther than the city, so Dad had to borrow a truck and trailer, drive into the city, and make two trips to haul the parts back to the radio station property. Then he and Mr. Houk painted the sections before beginning the assembly.

Fortunately, the sections for this tower were lighter than the ones Dad and the men in Costa Rica had wrestled to reach the heights in their assembly work there. Even so, the work was hard and dangerous, especially because of frequent high winds. We were all grateful to God that so far no one had been injured—other than Lizbeth's asthma attack brought on by inhaling some of the fumes emitted by the painting.

Meanwhile, YNOL had a very dedicated board of directors to oversee the ministry, and the women's auxiliary, called "Co-laborers with Christ," was a vital ministry to the station. Each lady carried a receipt book for donations to the station collected from members of their churches. Many denominations were supporting the station sacrificially. The radio station YNOL, ONDAS DE LUZ (Waves of Light) studios, transmitter, and tower were all built on the same property as the mud hut. It was at about this same time that Mom got word that her mother was not doing well—she might not have much more time.

Also at about this same time Dad bought the old British Ford taxi that had long sat idle on the station property. He paid $300 dollars, knowing that he'd have to make some repairs on the vehicle. While repairing the brakes, he got a drop of brake fluid in one eye. He cried out in pain even though we washed it out with water. But it didn't slow him down, he just kept working.

They finished assembling the tower—lights, guy wires and all—on September 3, and what a day of rejoicing it was—the work was complete, and no one had suffered any serious injury!

Another Ministry Trip

A week after the tower completion, Dad was on the road again, with Jim Houk. They drove to Panama and then caught a plane to Cali, Columbia, for a radio conference. Following that, they flew to a meeting at HCJB in Quito, Ecuador. They were gone just over two weeks, but, as usual when one of our parents was gone, two weeks seemed like an eternity.

But we weren't just lonely, we were a bit frightened, even though we knew God was in control. As we prepared for Dad's departure, Mom wrote,

> *It is going to be lonely, and I know you will pray for us. There have been three murders in three consecutive weeks, and the latest* [issue] *is threatening phone calls. We know that our heavenly Father watches over us.*

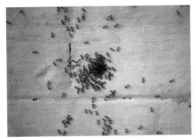

We and the ants fought an ongoing battle for control of our house near Managua.

To make matters worse, the night before Dad was to leave, the ants with whom we battled intermittently for control of the house, went into full attack mode. They infested our beds and bit us mercilessly—especially little David Lloyd, whose bed was situated directly beneath a large window, which was their primary point of attack. We'd have to counterattack the following morning without our general, Dad, who had no choice but to leave us, praying as he went.

Then, if all that wasn't bad enough, about a week after Dad's return from the Colombia and Peru trip, he had to leave a week later for a three-week trip to the States to get the new transmitter. We made do.

Chapter Eleven

Waves of Light

ଔ

By mid March of the new decade (1960), the YNOL antenna had been erected, Dad had installed the new high-power transmitter, and everyone involved with the station was working feverishly to complete the details for the dedication ceremony. Mom, Dad, the Holts, and the Houks worked almost non-stop, sometimes even through the night, painting, cleaning, making curtains, building cabinets, and doing anything else they could to make certain the station would be ready.

On March 12, Mom wrote,

We had the dedication for the YNOL (Waves of Light) radio station and the 15,000 watt transmitter, and over 1,000 attended. Some of our missionaries from Costa Rica also came. After the outdoor program we allowed everyone to enter the station, and then when they exited through the front door we gave them a free Pepsi. It seems that people here go crazy over something free. They were just wild. We had 40 cases of 24 bottles and we told them that they did not get one unless they went through the station first. They were like sharks after a man. They would grab the drink right out of our hands. We learned that one woman had four bottles in the bus, ready to take home. David was just sweating it out as they swarmed him with the case of Pepsi. We all vowed, "Never Again."

Over the following two weeks Dad often drove to outlying areas to test the YNOL reception. He was pleased with the results. In fact, by later in the same month we heard from listeners from as far away as

Texas, Colorado, and even back home in Pennsylvania. YNOL was the most powerful long-wave station in Latin America, commercial or religious. But soon the Catholic Church publicized that they were going to build a 25,000-watt station.

Extended Stay in Managua

It was a good thing that the YNOL station was doing so well, because not long after that the LAM mission board asked Dad and the rest of us to stay longer than we'd originally been told. Mom wrote, *"I guess we can't expect a change from this heat and dust and dirt."* We missed our home in Costa Rica, but, again, we took it in stride.

Later that month Dad had to make another trip, leavings us back in Managua while he was in El Salvador, visiting Assembly of God missionaries who were producing a gospel TV program every Sunday night. Dad consulted with them, gave them advice, and began broadcasting their radio program on YNOL.

Right after Dad returned from El Salvador he trained me to run the radio board (record players, tapes: mixer). I was not quite twelve, but I was conscientious; Dad knew he could trust me. So one night, when he had to be at a meeting, he left me in charge. Everything was going well until about the time Dad returned.

I went out to the main room to take a tape off the shelf for the next program, and that was when I felt a sharp pain in my hand. I kept looking at my hand and didn't see anything, but it sure hurt. In God's providence Daddy walked in at that moment, and I said, "Daddy something has stung me or bitten me in the hand and it hurts so much."

Daddy went to the shelf and looked into the slot where the tape had been and he found a five-inch-long scorpion! Its poison started to affect my body. Besides the pain in my hand, my tongue felt like it was swelling, and when I walked my legs felt numb. Daddy had me lie down at home and he took over the programs. I recovered after a night's rest.

In April "Evangelism in Depth" started with campaigns in six major centers in Nicaragua. We went to some of the meetings and also checked on the reception of YNOL, even up in the mountains of Jinotega. At the meetings Mother played the violin and Dad helped with the amplifying system. Many were saved during these meetings.

A few days after that Mom had the joy of taking a short trip to Costa Rica by herself to relax, visit old friends, and shop for YNOL radio parts. She was also there for the dedication of Nazareth Chapel, since we had a part in starting the church and building the facility. In addition, because she had learned that we would be in Nicaragua until February 1961, she went through trunks to get some clothes to bring back for my siblings and me. Unfortunately, that was also about the time that we children contracted chicken pox.

In May Mom wrote of little Mark,

> Mark is so funny as he tries to talk a lot, and many times you can't understand what he's saying, and he goes on for the longest time, making motions with his hands and mouth trying to get it out. He sucks his thumb and hugs his little cushion, feeling and rubbing it between his fingers. He's so sweet. David says he's the joy of our old age!

It was already stiflingly hot in May, and then the rainy season began, giving us sweltering levels of humidity. To make matters worse, the humidity gave the bugs—and the ever-present ants—new incentive to invade our house. We had size, strength, and insecticides on our side. They had stealth, tenacity, and unbelievable numbers going for them. We might kill a few dozen—or even a few hundred—of them, but those casualties would quickly be replaced by hundreds more. And so it went.

On May 23, 1960, Mom wrote,

> Today we are having the Geislers, Carol Sommers and the Sharers from Bluefields over for dinner. Charlie Sharer has an infection in his ear, so he came here to see a specialist. Carol is expecting and came for a check-up. Saturday we had a big rally and that finished the first phase of Evangelism in Depth. Now the churches must keep doing follow up with new believers to see the Lord's blessing.

My parents, the Houks, Don Paco, and other board members were committed to visiting two to three churches on Sundays to present the work of YNOL and solicit funds to keep the ministry going. That meant that our family of seven had to get up early to leave at 8 A.M. to make it through some Sunday schools and church services, where my Dad would present the needs of the new station, especially for extra tubes to make the output stronger.

Twelve Years Old

For my twelfth birthday Grandma and Grandpa Solt sent me this note:

You are now 12 years old. Our first grandchild is getting to be such a young lady. How we thank God that you are such a big help to your mother and daddy and sisters and brothers. You are now old enough to understand that life is more than play and fun. There are jobs to be done. There is work and sharing or toil to make not only others happy, but it also brings joy to us as we do it. God has placed us here in this world for a purpose. Your mother and daddy are used by God in spreading the good news of salvation to many living in darkness. They also have the joy of raising children to love God. You too, Lois, are here in this world to make others happy and to show them how a child of God should live. I know that you want to do this. But we need God's help and strength to be able to please Him. Every day we should pray "O Lord, help me to live for Thee." There will be problems. There will be hard places, but He has promised to help you, so He will.

We love you and like to get letters from you. Happy Birthday

Much love and many kisses, Grandma and Grandpa Solt

God's Provision

By mid July Dad had finished his construction of the much-appreciated two-room addition to our house. About that same time he killed an iguana that had entered the house without permission—probably hunting our insect intruders. Perhaps we should have espoused the philosophy that says, "The enemy of my enemy [the bugs] is my friend," but we really couldn't abide the thought of a wild iguana as our permanent house guest. So we killed it and gave it to some neighbors, who cooked it and offered some of it to us. It wasn't bad.

In mid August, Mother's sixth pregnancy caused her more stress, so she went to Dr. Pixley for a check-up, and he said the baby had dropped two inches and to be prepared for anything. Mom had resigned herself to having the baby in Nicaragua because she did not want to stay away from the family. Meanwhile, Libet and Mark were both having trouble with asthma, especially during the rainy season when everything was moldy.

Joannah (Juanita) and Gregg were helping Dad paint the tower. Joannah was not afraid of heights, so she was a big help up on the tower. One day, Dad interviewed the two of them on the tower, using a little portable tape recorder. Dad sometimes took their dinner up to them as they worked on the tower, and one day the wind was so strong it blew the rice off the fork before Gregg could get it in his mouth!

By late summer we were getting reports that people were receiving the YNOL signal as far north as Washington on the west coast and Massachusetts on the east coast. Dad was pleased by those reports. Unfortunately, the funds needed to keep the station functioning properly were not quite keeping pace with the station's many wonderful accomplishments. But my parents were confident that God would continue to provide.

One More Solt

On September 17, 1960, at 11 in the morning, after Mom had been in labor less than two hours, John Jacob joined the Solt family. He weighed eight pounds, nine ounces, and Mom said he looked just like Mark. We were all very excited by the new arrival, and Lillian and I got things ready for Mom and our new baby brother. The total hospital bill for John's birth was $154, and the mission insurance paid $75 of that, so my parents had to pay just $79. Oh, how things have changed since then!

Ten days after John's arrival, Mom wrote,

> It was thirteen year ago that our feet landed on Costa Rican soil. How happy these years have been serving the Lord in the places of His choosing. Psalm 24 says, "If it had not been the Lord who was on our side...the stream had gone over our soul." When we left the States we were alone, but among the other numerous blessings, the Lord has seen fit to give us six precious little Jewels. The children have been on vacation for two weeks and have been thoroughly enjoying taking care of baby John.

78

Floods

Heavy rains began near the end of October. By the last day of the month, after eleven straight days of rain, we'd had nine inches of rain and flood waters inundated much of the area. Roads were in bad shape, and some bridges were washed away. The Red Cross brought flood relief services, and our YNOL broadcasts asked all evangelical churches to join in the relief efforts. My parents were very much involved in the efforts. Dad even drove around and collected relief supplies to take to the relief workers.

Libet's Leg

In mid November Lizbeth (we often called her Libet) jumped from the fender of a stationary car and re-injured her hip. X-rays determined that the hip had healed properly from the previous injury, so doctors began to think that the problem was tuberculosis in the hip bone. She was once again put in a full-leg cast.

The next day Dad barely made it home from the city before the traffic was backed up for miles when fourteen revolutionaries took 250 school girls as hostages. Eventually the rebels surrendered to the authorities and all the girls were freed.

On the nineteenth, Libet returned home from the hospital—this time in a full body cast. I felt bad for my poor little sister, but she took it all pretty well. She stayed in my parents' air-conditioned bedroom. It's a good thing she was there, because one day, at about that time, Mom walked into the back bedroom and found a neighbor's cow had walked through an open door and was standing next to the bed.

Three Miracles

Around the time of Thanksgiving, Mom wrote of three miracles of salvation:

> *Two were our own precious jewels. Lloyd seems to have had a real experience, with tears, repenting especially for the way he treats Mommy and Daddy. I was alone when I dealt with him, and I asked if he had ever accepted the Lord. He said, "No but I pray every night." Then one day in the hospital, when we had our*

devotions, Libet and I, she was kind of restless and then we talked about trusting the Lord and she said that she had never accepted Him. So she did too. Yesterday the little neighbor girl sent a note and said she wanted to accept the Lord so I dealt with her and she also accepted Jesus. Pray for each of these.

Another Visit

Grandma and Grandpa Solt arrived for their six-week Christmas / New Year's visit, and were we ever excited—and not just for the gifts they brought! They had to get accustomed to the bugs that the rainy season had chased into our house—as well as the rats and bats and other creatures that made everyday life in Managua such an adventure.

A visit from Grandpa and Grandma Solt was occasion for celebration.

The year ended on a sad note when Central American missionary Bill Ballie had a fatal accident. He was up on a ladder, working on some electrical wires at the radio station in Guatemala. He was shocked, fell off the ladder and ruptured a vessel in his neck and died. We prayed for his family.

Chapter Twelve

Waves of Heat

CB

After a six-week visit, Grandma and Grandpa Solt were preparing to return to the New Year's cold in Pennsylvania. We were really sad at the thought of their departure, as were they. Although they'd probably welcome the cold—and even the Pennsylvania snow—after the incessant Managua heat and dust.

At about the same time that Grandma and Grandpa were preparing to leave, astronaut Alan Shepherd was training for his trip to outer space. His training required him to endure temperature extremes for relatively short periods—temperatures as hot as 130 Fahrenheit! We laughed: Managua has temperatures as high as 120 for days, weeks, or even months at a time. On top of that, Lisbeth had to endure two months of that heat in her full-body cast and then hobble around on crutches. What a little trooper she was.

But we knew the sacrifices were worth it when we heard stories like this one, in 1961: Another evangelical missionary was preaching at an open-air meeting when the mayor told him he'd have to stop because all the people in the town were Roman Catholics. Soon another city official came along and contested with the mayor. He told the missionary that he had listened to YNOL and was taking a correspondence course after he had accepted Jesus as Savior. Hallelujah!

Lisbeth Leaves and Lillian Gets 'Skinned'

In April, when the Holts returned to the States, they took Lisbeth to stay with Grandma and Grandpa Solt so that she could escape the heat and dust that aggravated her asthma—and so that she could gain some weight, she'd gotten quite thin. The rest of us would join her there for another furlough in August, though she didn't know that.

Lisbeth missed some excitement not long after her departure. In the middle of the night baby John needed a change. Mom reached into a drawer and pulled out a clean diaper, never giving the action a second thought. The next morning, in the light of day, when she again opened that same drawer, she spotted a coral snake coiled up in a corner, inches from where she'd grabbed the diaper a few hours before. Coral snakes have a powerful and often fatal venom, but, fortunately, they're not very aggressive. But they're certainly not passive enough to keep as a house pet, so Dad killed it.

Not long after that incident, I saw Lillian out in the back field, by the tower. She was yelling, and I thought she was playing with me. Finally I realized that she was calling in pain. She'd gone out to play with a calf and the rope tied to the animal wound around one of Lillian's leg. As the calf ran, the rope—loose enough to come free but just tight enough to rub with tremendous friction—scraped off a couple layers of skin. So Lillian's calf was skinned by a calf—ironic.

El Salvador Next?

In late spring, Dad went to El Salvador to investigate the possibilities of setting up another nationally owned and operated Christian radio station like YNOL. The interest was great and things moved along faster than expected. One man donated his small commercial station and another couple offered a small piece of land and a building to house the station temporarily. Some locals formed a Club TRES (Three), which in Spanish is "Tranmisiones Radiales Evangelicas Salvadoraneas" and pledged to pay three colones per month to support the station.

Family Reunion

In July we flew to Miami and then drove north to Allentown, to stay with Dad's parents. Their house was large, and we filled it with the noise and running feet of six children: Lois, 13; Lillian, 12; Libet, 11; Lloyd, 8; Mark, 5; and John, almost 1 year old. We hadn't seen Libet since April, so we allowed baby John to go in the house first and Libet thought he looked familiar—like her brother John! Then she screamed when she saw all of us! (She never had a very quiet voice.) It was hard to leave my grandparents' home in August and go north to Syracuse, New York. A Christian professor from the University allowed us to rent their four-bedroom house for the winter at only $50 per month plus utilities. We were very comfortable and happy with the arrangement. My parents were full of praise to the Lord for His goodness to us once again.

Dad spent much of the furlough time in classes that would benefit the mission work. Mom also took some classes and worked with Dad on an audio/visual instruction project, which is the greatest need for our mission in Latin America. We children had a great time and even enjoyed our music lessons. Libet and Lillian took violin lessons, Lloyd took trombone and I took piano and organ.

Dad bought a thirty-six-foot-long travel trailer that we'd haul along and place in El Salvador when we returned at the end of the furlough. It was cheap—it would need a lot of work, and provide some real adventures as we worked to get it safely to its intended destination.

Down the Pan-American Highway
After nearly a year in the States, in April 1962, it was time to return to Central America. And what it trip it would be: two adults piloting two vehicles, packed full of kids and belongings—and hauling a huge trailer down the long and sometimes treacherous Pan-American Highway. But we'd barely started when we had to stop because of gale-force winds along the Pennsylvania Turnpike.

When we finally resumed, with Grandma and Grandpa along to help for much of the drive, my parents took turns: Dad drove the fully packed pickup truck hauling the huge trailer, while Mom drove the station wagon, packed with belongings and kids. It wasn't long before more annoyances began to strike. First, Dad had to change a flat tire on each of the vehicles. Then the trailer door kept opening and flapping in the breeze. After Dad wired the door shut the distractions eased up for a while as we made our way southwest, toward the crossing into Mexico, at Nogales.

One evening, when we couldn't find a suitable park for the night, we pulled up to a little white church and discovered that the pastor had been a classmate of my parents from Bible School! He allowed us to plug into their electricity and water as well as use their bathroom. In the morning they even filled our gas tanks. We praised the Lord for His love and provision!

We chose to cross the border at Nogales because it was near the coastal road, which had the fewest mountains. We bought food at a supermarket and then crossed the border into Mexico. Grandpa and Grandma stayed with us until Ciudad Obregon, where they bought tickets to fly back.

At Culiacan, the capital of the state of Sinaloa, we crossed the river by a concrete causeway, which is passable only during the dry season. It was very steep getting down and out since the river was on either side of us. If it had been in the rainy season this causeway would have been under water. We crossed several other narrow bridges that there were only inches wider than the trailer. Mazatlan was a welcome spot for all of us children because we got to swim in the Gulf of California while Dad made some repairs on the trailer.

We had reached that precarious point I wrote about in the opening of the book. We made it through, as you know, but only by God's grace and with plenty of help.

After picking our way slowly through El Tapon (The Cork), we arrived at a stretch of new highway, leading into Guatemala City. The

We threaded the needle through "The Cork."

highway was, however, still under construction. Dad persuaded the construction supervisor to allow us to proceed, with the understanding that we would drive slowly and carefully so that the new asphalt would not pull up. We obeyed and drove very near the edge. But that caused a problem when the house trailer got stuck in the soft sand right above a fifty-foot culvert. Bulldozers pulled us out, though Dad was concerned that the trailer hitch would snap. But praise God, all held and we pulled out.

We finally arrived in El Salvador in mid-May and promptly began setting up the trailer as our "base camp." But on June 22, Dad took Lillian and me with him as he returned to Nicaragua to make repairs at YNOL radio station. Then we were allowed to accompany him to a two-week television workshop in Costa Rica. Pretty exciting stuff for two sisters barely in their teens.

Meanwhile, Lisbet had recovered sufficiently to help Mom with cleaning and caring for the younger kids.

YSHQ Begins

Later that summer, we had the official opening of the radio station YSHQ in El Salvador. We hosted a tamale supper for all the pastors and

Work on the trailer house in El Salvador was progressing.

members of the board. Forty-two attended, and one of the men gave a testimony of how the Lord led him to give the old station and frequency to YSHQ. Dad told how the Lord provided so many pieces of equipment and what they still needed before we could get on the air. He also showed slides of the work at YNOL so that they would be encouraged.

On August 6, Carol Walz, a teacher from North Syracuse, back in the States, arrived. God had called her to come to El Salvador to teach the Solt children—us! She was a wonderful teacher, and we felt honored that God sent her to us.

Dad spent most of August in Guatemala helping with Evangelism in Depth. They held campaigns in twenty-five towns, from one end of the country to the other. He used our truck with much of the equipment that had been donated in the States. Four college boys traveled with him, and they went into the remote areas, showing films and paving the way for the regional campaigns. They showed the films forty-one times in parks, schools, and churches, reaching about 25, 000 people. Many heard the gospel message for the first time.

In September, Mother flew to Lima, Peru, for a radio conference. She went because Dad felt that the YSHQ work should be represented and he'd been gone too often over the past months. Meanwhile, we kids stayed home and continued our studies.

Working With Hermano Pablo … and a New Home

Yes, we actually enjoyed our little school.

In October 1962 my parents were working with Paul Finkenbinder, better known as *Hermano Pablo*, and filming a Spanish-language biblical drama called *Barabbas*. Dad was the camera and sound man. The crew sometimes had to do a scene as many as seven times before they got it right. Because most of the untrained cast of native Salvadorians was employed during the day, they filmed at night in an old, empty warehouse. Sometimes Dad and Mom wouldn't arrive home until five A.M. They said that when the crowd of actors shouted "Crucify Him," they heard rocks hit the warehouse roof. From then on the actors whispered during the rehearsals until time for the actual shooting. This was the first Spanish-language gospel television film to be produced with a Latin cast. After finishing that film, they again worked with Hermano Pablo to produce a film based on Matthew's Gospel.

We finally moved to our home's new location, which was only five minutes from the radio station. We were in the same compound as the Houk family. Our thirty-six-foot trailer was moved to the center of San Salvador, near the Houks. We helped Dad build an eleven-by-thirty-five-foot-long room, and we completed it in just two days! Then we waited for Horace Holt to come and do the divisions and finishing work. This gave us three extra rooms. After that we put up curtains to keep out the dust and to block the view of "peeping Toms." Next we built a roof over the trailer and the addition, so it seemed a little like a tree house. Then we had to spend two days digging a ditch for the sewer, but it was hard work because we had big shady trees with huge roots that made the digging rough. Carol, Lillian and I did a good amount of the digging too, because the hired man hardly did anything. We were really sore over the next few days. But we had plenty of shade, and my parents were very happy with the location.

Our building duties weren't finished: We also helped Dad build a two-room school house right next to our trailer. That was where Carol taught us—the Solt children and a few other missionary kids—traditional subjects, along with art and sewing, and even manners. We put on school programs with painted backgrounds and sang in a chorus. God used Carol and her parents to bless the children at the San Salvador Christian Academy.

We all pitched in on preparing our new school.

Chapter Thirteen

Moving Forward in Ministry

CR

In El Salvador in the early 60s, a self-igniting oven was virtually unheard of. Mom was grateful to have a gas stove at all. During one day of baking Mom went to light the oven, not realizing that the gas had been on for some time. The floating layer of gas exploded and burned her hands, arms, and face. Fortunately, most of the burns were not severe, but she kept her hand in ice water for a while. She had blisters on her fingers and arms, but she was grateful that she'd been in front of us children, shielding us from any harm.

Revolution and Routine

In late November 1962, my parents left us in El Salvador while they went to Guatemala (five hours away) for the final meeting of Evangelism in Depth, which was to be followed by a parade. But the morning of the parade a mini-revolution took place and everyone was on edge. Some disgruntled army officers launched a guerrilla war against the military government, and the government responded in force. My parents saw the planes opening fire on their targets as well as dropping rockets and strafing. One bomb was thrown from a car and exploded in a wall near the Union Church.

They decided to go on with the parade and there were many beautiful floats, along with their car adorned with a sign on top declaring, "YSHQ, Radio Progreso, Your Evangelical Radio Station from El Salvador."

About 30,000 attended the final meeting and even the president was present with his cabinet.

A bit like Forrest Gump, my parents often seemed to find themselves in the midst of intense action—but always with God's angels looking out for them.

As they drove back they had a blowout. Dad removed the spare tire from the back of the car and it bounced out on the highway and then in one big leap it went down over a big cliff into a swampy river below. Dad went down to retrieve the tire and returned with his shoes thoroughly soaked with water. We thanked the Lord that it did not go into the center of the river.

In December Dad returned to the States for two weeks to get things for the station and our schooling. My parents wrote to their friends and said that the most urgent need was money for the transmitter, for station equipment, and for the tower that my Dad was going to ship from the states, as well as for the construction of the radio station. The land had been leveled off and was paid for. The studio/transmitter building plans were being drawn up and soon would be submitted to the government for approval.

After Dad returned, we began visiting local churches, sharing about the ministry of YSHQ. We went to a Baptist church about two hours' drive from home. We wondered how any church so far from a population center could prosper. We were surprised to find a large beautiful church, with about 400 present. Carol Walz, our school teacher from North Syracuse, drew a chalk drawing of the city of San Salvador and its towering volcanoes, and then, when the black light came on, everyone could only see the cross, with the YSHQ station and tower. It reminded my parents over and over that God was faithful and that someday soon we would be on the air with the Good News.

Another little church was held in a farm house. People came and we met under the porch. With sheep cows, ducks, and dogs meandering nearby, the people listened intently as my parents presented the ministry of this new radio station. When we left, a pig was sprawled out lazily, blocking the road, so Dad inched the car closer and pushed it. The hog then stood and its mass lifted the front of our car a bit off the ground!

On another trip back from Jinotepe to San Salvador it was pouring rain and we (Mother, Dad, baby John, and me) were in a small English Anglia. Dad could hardly see a few feet in front of him. With no time to react, he saw a horse standing in the middle of the road. We smashed into the animal and sent him up over the car, taking off our CB antenna. The front windshield shattered into small pieces and Dad's hand was bleeding. In those days cars had no seat belts. We were on the side of the road and I thought baby John had died. I shook and shook him, calling his name! Finally he sleepily opened his eyes and we realized he was okay. One of the board members of YSHQ, Dr. Arragon, a physician, was just behind us and he stopped and checked us all out. Praise God we were all fine.

Grandma Goes Home and Our Work Continues

Nineteen sixty-three moved along in a mostly routine manner until late April, when Grandma DiValentino died. We weren't surprised, she was nearly 81, and had been in ill health, but losing a loved one—even one who has gone to be with the Lord—is never easy. It's okay to mourn, but, as the apostle Paul wrote to the Thessalonians, "We do not want you to be uninformed, brethren, about those who are asleep, so that you will not grieve as do the rest who have no hope." Grandma DiValentino came to faith in Jesus late in her life, but despite her late confession of faith, she was just as saved as anyone who trusts Jesus.

Grandma and Grandpa Solt attended the funeral, back in Meyersdale, and then wrote a long letter with the details, and they enclosed a little flower for my mother. Mom then wrote this note:

> If letters could be memorials, then this is one I would like to dedicate to my parents and their help in my Christian life. Though they did not come to know the Lord until late in life, they never objected to my dedicating my life to the Lord on the mission field. Pray that we would not be hindrances to our children's service in the Lord's vineyard.

As the construction work on the station and the tower continued, my mother and aunt Ginny Houk had meetings with local women to keep them interested in the radio work. The station was supported by all the evangelical denominations, and the women had societies to help raise funds. Some of the churches in the city had buildings along huge ravines that were formed by erosion. Thousands of people lived in little shacks along these ravines. The adobe churches were small but would squeeze almost 100 inside. At one meeting the women wanted to buy a foot of the tower (for eight dollars), so they took an offering, which was short by two dollars. Some ladies walked to the platform and gave a few more pennies and before long we were praising the Lord that they had passed the goal!

YSHQ on Air!
On July 17, 1963, Mom wrote the following:

> Yesterday, at 3 PM, we yelled, "Alleluia, praise the Lord." We got the 1,000-watt RCA transmitter out of customs and got it located in its place in the transmitter room at the station. You can imagine our happiness after waiting so many months. We don't know why it was detained so long. We are working hard to get on the air. There are several more shipments still in customs and the tower is there plus the tape recorders. The people move so slowly here. We did get an exemption from duty. Praise the Lord for all He has done!

Two days later, the transmitter was on and transmitting a test signal with a provisional antenna. We were filled with praise as we heard the message of salvation going out over the air. We transmitted on 1330 kilocycles, and we were assigned a power of 5,000 watts (as soon as the Lord provides a stronger transmitter).

Meanwhile, the rains were very heavy, so building the 200-foot tower was delayed. The tower was finished July 24. Dad then taught Lillian and me how to work the controls, and we did so from six to noon, once the station began temporary broadcasting.

A Brief Return to Costa Rica
In late August our whole family made a brief trip to Costa Rica for radio ministry meetings, and God provided a missionary home for us so that we could all be together. Paul Pretiz was doing a very good job, but it seemed that he was overextended. The Kinches were expecting baby number eleven, and they invited all the missionary children in the area (those who were home from school in the States). They had a full house,

and Aunt Esther seemed a little tired. She made her delicious cinnamon buns and donuts. We had meetings and doctors' appointments while in San Jose.

We took some of the Kinch boys and visited the volcano Irazu, which appeared to be becoming increasingly active. Clouds clung to the mountainside as we drove toward the belching cone. When we reached the crater we could hear rocks being thrown out, and some of them were really hot to touch! With

The Irazu volcano crater is beautiful-- when it's in a good mood.

all the ash, vegetation was dying near the volcano and the area around it looked terrible. As we descended the mountain the falling ash sounded like rain, and Dad had to turn on the windshield wipers so he could see well enough to stay on the road.

The streets of San Jose had piles of black ash, which the people had to clean out of the drains. People were getting frantic. They couldn't even hang up laundry outside because the ash fell so heavily.

We saw a terrible accident on the way home. A Jeep had rolled over, and a little girl who'd been inside was pinned underneath it. A group of men lifted it up to get her out, but they had to hurry before the police arrived. The Costa Rican police routinely jailed anyone involved in any way with an accident. (My parents were told to scram if they ever were in an accident.) This was the sad thing about this accident: A man was there who could have offered assistance, but he said his hands were tied because he could be accused of causing the accident and be taken to jail. The little girl was breathing hard and unconscious in her mother's arms when we left.

Return to El Salvador—and the Perilous Routine
After our return from Costa Rica, we had to work hard to finish the tower in time for the official opening of the station, which was set for September 1. Even we older Solt kids helped, sometimes climbing the tall tower (wearing safety harnesses). Once, Lillian got shocked while

she was 100 feet high on the tower. Thank God for the harness. It was exciting work.

Paul Pretiz and a few others were scheduled to come from Costa Rica for the celebration.

Following Bill Ballie's death, Mrs. Baillie came to live on the compound with us in San Salvador, so my Dad had three women care for: Mom, Ginny Houk, and Helen Bailie (in addition to all the Solt children). My Dad was only in his thirties when many of his missionary friends died. That had an effect on his life. (I think back now to hearing stories of nineteenth-century missionaries who took their coffins along when they were assigned to far-away countries, because they didn't expect to return alive.) Dad said, "I've got to work harder; I don't know how much time I have left!" I remember him dictating to my mother his wishes, and instructions for how to deal with his death. She was weeping while she did this. He wanted us to be taken care of, so he made her aware of his wishes even though he was only in his thirties.

A Heroic Teen—and Routine Life as Teens

Irazu isn't the only volcano in Latin America—the continent is loaded with them. In 1964, when I was sixteen, I was one of ten teens who went on a hike up the Izalco volcano, in western El Salvador. Izalco was officially listed as an active volcano, but at the time it was not erupting, and it seemed to be in a calm state. The ascent was steep and potentially dangerous, as the surface was covered with small, loose gravel that had pelted the area during previous eruptions.

Imagine sliding down this mountain to save a friend.

All of us made it safely to the top. It seemed that the descent would be easier than the climb. But the loose gravel gave way under the feet of one of the other girls, Cathy, sending her sliding and then tumbling uncontrollably down the rugged mountainside. After the rest of us carefully made our way down to her, we found that she was unconscious and appeared to be badly bruised and

93

lacerated. We didn't know if she had any broken bones. And we still had a long way to reach the bottom of the mountainside.

We did know she wouldn't be able to descend the mountain under her own power. And, as steep as the mountainside was—along with the tricky footing resulting from the loose gravel—we also knew no one would be able to carry her down safely. One of the boys, Mark Nicodemus, a big sixteen-year-old came up with an innovative, though self-sacrificing, plan: He would cradle her in his arms, but rather than trying to stand to carry her, he'd slide down on his posterior. He made it, safely, but at the expense of a severely lacerated backside.

Our team leader had gone ahead to get help, and at about six in the evening, he returned with several local men and a hammock. When they got Cathy into the nearby town and examined her, they learned that she had no broken bones—praise the Lord!

We all admired Mark for his bravery in risking himself to help Cathy. But, as teens, we often admired the opposite gender for attributes that had nothing to do with bravery. We girls had "boy crushes," which sometimes caused confrontations with our parents. Liz once threatened to leave home because Mom and Dad wouldn't allow her to date Luis, whom she liked very much. Lizbeth, Lillian, and I all had a crush on Omar Mejia, a young and upcoming concert pianist who was a Christian. I guess we were like most teens, seeing ourselves as adults, but in many ways still very childlike.

Disciplines: Solt Orchestra
Not only did my parents take us to lakes, pools, and volcanoes for outdoor activities but they also introduced us to the discipline of musical instruments. We had to practice several times a week, which we didn't always enjoy. Then we would play in different churches where the radio ministry was presented or on furlough. Mother, Lillian and

The Solts are a musical family.

94

Lizbeth played violins and I played piano and organ. Dad and Mark played trumpet and Lloyd played trombone. When Mark was little he played the triangle and John played a bell. We took music lessons at the San Salvador Conservatory free of charge and were exposed to good classical music. This added a whole new dimension to our lives.

Chapter Fourteen

Shaken, but Not Moved

cx

On May 3, 1965, we were nearly shaken from our beds as the ground beneath us heaved and jerked violently—as it had done many times before and would do again often in the future in this earthquake-prone part of the world.

As the trailer bucked and bounced, closet doors opened and slammed, lights flickered and extinguished, and virtually every loose item in the house fell and either shattered or rolled uncontrollably, we prayed—and trembled.

Earthquakes are not uncommon in El Salvador.

While trailer homes have many disadvantages, one upside is that, because they merely rest on the ground's surface rather than being attached to it, as are "traditional" houses, they have some "give." When the earth beneath them begins to "dance," they're loose enough to dance along rather than trying to stubbornly stand their ground (a futile effort during a massive quake). Dad understood this phenomenon, so he told us to just stay in our beds and ride it out. The result was that, while the 6.3-level quake killed 125 precious Salvadorian souls and leveled thousands of homes, leaving 48,000 people homeless, by God's grace, we came through uninjured and with minimal damage to our home.

El Salvador was our adopted home; my parents could have let the quake chase us back to Pennsylvania, but they were certain God had called us to minister to the people of Central America. This was no time to quit. Dad carefully cleaned up all the broken glass, then he let the rest of us get up and help with all the other cleaning. Life would go on, and our ministry would continue.

School was a major part of our routine life in El Salvador. Mom and Dad didn't want to send us to the big missionary school in Honduras, so, as I mentioned before, we built our own little two-room schoolhouse right next to our trailer house. Over the years, we had several different teachers, including Carol Walz, Rose Ann Murphy, and Grace Richardson. One year, Grandpa and Grandma Solt were our teachers.

Another Furlough—Extended for Me

In June, after the school year ended, we flew to Miami for another furlough. Grandpa and Grandma had left their car at the Miami airport for us, so we piled in and drove north.

For me, the biggest event of the furlough came as our time in the States ended. While the other members of our family, along with Harriet Kassay of Easton, Pennsylvania, who would be the new missionary school teacher, began the long drive back to El Salvador, I stayed behind, with the Richard Edwards family, friends from North Syracuse Baptist Church. All the members of the Edwards family were kind to me, and I appreciated their hospitality while allowing me to spend my senior year of high school in the States, but I cried sometimes nonetheless—I missed my family.

After attending tiny missionary schools in Central America for so long, the huge, modern high school in New York was almost overwhelming. Fortunately, the school principal, Paul Wagner, a Christian, had kept my parents up to date with the academic requirements I needed to complete prior to that year, so I was ready scholastically. Still, socially and culturally, it was a huge adaptation. (But, praise God, Ardith Edwards Olsen has remained a dear friend since that year.)

Another Drive Down the Pan-Am Highway

Meanwhile, the other members of the Solt family, along with Harriet, drove south, with Dad and three of the kids in the Falcon. Mom, Harriet and the remaining kids crammed into the little British Anglia, which they nicknamed "Puddles" because it leaked so badly that the kids played in the puddles that formed on the car's floor as they drove through many rainstorms.

In Mexico, they had to traverse a 6,500-foot summit before descending into Saltillo. Obviously, the road was not lighted, so the foggy, nighttime drive was harrowing. Harriet and Libet kept their heads out the windows trying to help Mom see her way along the long stretches of winding mountain roads devoid of protective railings. As they drove, they continued to call on the Lord, and eventually He lifted the fog so that they could continue safely to Saltillo.

After a chaotic drive through Mexico City, a night at the Central American Mission Bible Institute, a sleepless night parked next to a truckload of smelly, squealing, grunting pigs, more treacherous mountain roads, heavy rains and floods, flat-tire repairs, and just a lot of monotonous driving, they finally arrived at the El Salvador border at midnight, where the border guards ordered them to unload every suitcase for inspection.

Finally, at about 8 A.M., on September 29, they arrived home in El Salvador. Time to resume the routine life of a missionary family in Central America.

Mark Leaves His Mark

For eight-year-old Mark the routine included throwing rocks, as little boys love to do. He decided to toss one of those rocks over a sheet that was hanging in the carport. He'd forgotten, as little boys often do, that the family's Plymouth station wagon was parked behind the sheet. The shattered windshield would not be easily—or inexpensively—replaced in El Salvador—as he soon learned from our irate father.

Not appreciating his punishment, Mark tried, briefly, to run away from home. (Earlier in Costa Rica four-year-old Libet also packed her little suitcase and walked out the door.) Not long after this event one of us kids discovered how to get into the family safe, where Mom stored the peanut butter and chocolate. Quite a bit was consumed before we were discovered.

Growing Pains

Later that year, Paul Finkenbinder (Hermano Pablo) joined Dad and Mom at the YSHQ studios to film a movie based on Matthew's Gospel and then another based on the story of Queen Esther. Dad was behind the camera, and Mom handled the sound, while Brother Paul directed. Libet and Lillian had small parts, and Mark played Haman being hanged on the gallows he'd had built for Mordecai. I was sorry I missed it.

My parents worked with Hermano Pablo.

At about that same time, David Lloyd was recruited to serve as a translator at a camp. It sounded like a fun job, but it turned out to be a real pain. It was bad enough being away from home and family, but blistered feet from long walks while wearing holey socks, the copious mosquito bites, and the diarrhea from an unfamiliar diet really did make him an unhappy camper.

Even with my absence, the Solt teen-girl boy competition continued. While I was still in New York, Lillian wrote me this note:

The guy that Libet likes has a bad crush on me. Libet is so brokenhearted over this. It's not my fault. To tell the truth I like him too, but so she doesn't feel bad I'm not going to be his girlfriend. He has asked me to go out about 50 times!! Tomas is real cute, only I won't be his girlfriend either because I don't want to be tied down to one boy. You know me. I like Omar because he is the only guy I can talk to who will not talk about things like this. Margy Houk is just crazy about him and Libet likes him too. Let me know about your romantic life.

After graduating from North Syracuse High School, I returned to El Salvador to spend the summer with my family before leaving again, this time for nursing school. During that summer, a group of fifteen young people from the States came from World Gospel Crusades to distribute literature. Five of the boys stayed on to work in the radio building. They painted, laid sod, and put in a drainage system so we wouldn't have any more floods. Four of the guys stayed in our teacher's apartment and ate with us, which we girls didn't mind at all.

Dad spent some time that summer driving around the country, distributing radio receivers to evangelical families who lived in areas that had no pastor to lead them. The radios could receive only the YSHQ signal, so they heard all the Christian programs, and, as a result, many new congregations formed.

Off to Nursing School

In September 1966, when I was just 18, I returned to the States and enrolled in Grand View School of Nursing in Sellersville, Pennsylvania. I was one of just twenty-four in my class. The whole school had only seventy-two nursing students in three classes. We studied year round, with only four weeks of vacation in the summer. The whole course cost just $1,200—money my parents had saved since my birth. Every birthday and Christmas monetary gift was tucked away for college.

I studied very hard, sensing that God would lead me back to Central America as a missionary nurse, helping in villages where there are no clinics or doctors. My parents wrote to me every week and we also talked via ham radio, thanks to Dr. Peters at Grand View. I concentrated on surgical nursing so that I could do an appendectomy. I also focused in obstetrics so that I could deliver babies in remote areas. My room in the nursing residence was my "home," and it was the first time I had a bedroom to myself! Of course, I missed my sisters dearly.

In October I began to have second thoughts about my choice for a nursing education. Would I be wiser to go to a larger, more-recognized college? I shared that concern with my parents. They replied:

We feel sure that the Lord has led you there; however we think we should always be open to the Lord's leading. Remember that while you might not be getting the last word in training at the biggest school, we are sure that the contacts that you are making and the witness that you have will more than compensate for anything that you might miss. We are also sure that if you are at the top of your class you will have no trouble passing the nursing state exams to become a registered nurse. Just keep working hard and don't worry so much. It was good to talk to you this morning and hear all about your boyfriends. Just don't get too interested in them that you don't get your lessons done! You have had enough dates now until the end of the year!

As I went off to nursing school, Mom expected that I'd soon meet some young men, and marriage might enter my thoughts, so she wrote me this letter of advice:

First of all let me say that I had no one give me any special advice like I am giving to you, except the Lord answered my humble prayer and gave my sweetheart to me. There are so many factors to take into consideration that if I number them it doesn't really mean in that order of importance.

1. Do you know his/her family background? If it is stable, you have a good idea what your family life will be like. Are they lazy or do they get things done when they say, or not? Do they get up late or early? Which do you prefer? Do they watch a lot of TV, eat a lot, have hobbies, and recreation? Do they do things as a family or does each go his separate way? Do the children respect the parents? Is there a lot of arguing, etc? Is this really what you want in the life you will have with him here?

2. Do you really love him with all your heart? Is there some other one you compare him with and like maybe a little bit? Then you don't love him/her with all your heart. Is he the only one you want to be with, all others fade? Do you doubt his/her love or asking yourself, "Do I really love him, I don't know?" There will be no doubt or question in your mind and you will trust him/her. Remember you are giving away your whole life for better or for worse. No turning back even though it gets rough. Have you had arguments or have them often, then your romance isn't even for the birds! Do you both like to eat out or do things at home?

3. Do you enjoy doing the same things, like the same things, music, food, hobbies, radio programs, TV programs? Remember over the months and years these all become amplified. Same with a temper, does he/she get angry easily, impatient, sulk...for how long? Does he/she some or get ready on time or keep others waiting, does it annoy you?

4. Are you proud of him; do you hold them in high esteem? Do you consider him the final word in major decisions? Is he more intelligent and have more training than you? Do you have compatible occupations?

5. In your estimation does the Lord come first, loved one second? Have you asked the Lord and do you have perfect peace about it? If there is a shadow of doubt, then it is not the Lord's will. Is he or she committed 100% to the Lord for whatever He wants, missions, etc? Do you both put the same value on money? One cannot be frugal and the other spendthrift. ALL money and all your belongings are the Lord's.

Genuine love is essential to a happy marriage: 1 Corinthians 13 and Philippians 2

Close Calls in Guatemala

The day after Thanksgiving, in 1966, Dad, Mother, Ginny, Margie, Grace, and Rose Ann left for Guatemala; they had to get the car out of the country and get new visas to stay another three months. (Much of my parents' missionary life consisted of leaving a country every three months to get a new visa, rather than getting residency papers, which were very expensive.) They visited with the Shakelfords in Guatemala, but they didn't stay long. The government there had recently held an election and the people had chosen Julio Cesar Mendez Montenegro, the nation's first non-military president in decades. If they thought a civilian president would bring peace, they were wrong, as my parents saw firsthand.

The streets were torn up, so they could not park near the Shakelfords' home. As Dad got out of the car he heard two or three gunshots, so he ran quickly into the house. The next morning they all heard anti-aircraft artillery and machine guns firing nearby. Four policemen had been gunned down the day before.

In Antigua, after viewing the Mayan ruins, they visited a missionary whose car had been stolen the week before. While she and her two little girls were sitting in the station wagon and her husband was shopping, two men came with pistols and told her to hand over the keys and get out. She and her two daughters did as they were ordered, and the two

102

men drove away in the new car. Fortunately, this time, no one was hurt. No one ever said the life of a missionary is without adventures—and risks.

As I Prepare to Return for a Visit ...
About a month before I returned for a two-week visit with my family they experienced another El Salvador earthquake. Mom wrote, *"At 2:00 this morning we had a real good shaker, which woke up the whole family as well as all the dogs in the neighborhood."* Fortunately, the quake wasn't powerful to do too much damage to the new school building for missionary students being built nearby.

Shortly before my arrival the family drove back to Managua to install a new transmitter at the YNOL station. From there they drove back to Costa Rica to enjoy a few days at the coast before going to meetings and conferences at the LAM headquarters. Following the meetings, they returned home to continue the routine, and to wait for their oldest child to return. But they were waiting for more than my arrival; a group of forty-five volunteers from our home church, Bethany Bible Fellowship, in Hatfield, Pennsylvania, was scheduled to come and help us for a while.

Mom wrote the following in an August letter to supporters:

We would appreciate your special prayers for the YSHQ radio station finances. As you know, this missionary station is sponsored by the local Christians here and it has been a blessing to work with them and see how the Lord supplies from one month to another. However, the last two months have been rather discouraging as the funds have not come in as they should. Pray with us for those who have pledged to support the station but have been slack in fulfilling their promises. We have begun to visit the churches and individuals. It was a joy to visit one little old lady who does not have much in material possessions (a few chairs and her own bed), but on leaving she gave us a special offering of ten dollars. How this touched our hearts. This past week we helped with a radio course. Friday night we had a banquet and each student gave special thanks for our teaching them.

As I returned to the States to resume my nursing studies, I thanked God for allowing me to be a member of a family that He was using to bring many into His kingdom.

Late in 1967, Dad went to Lima, Peru, and made some important contacts that appeared likely to lead to some new areas of radio and/or TV ministry there. Waiting to see how God leads....

Chapter Fifteen

Furloughs, the New Ministry in Mexico, and Two Weddings

℺

The Salvadorian government priced my parents—and many other missionaries—right out of the country when they began to require them to pay $800 for each resident adult. In those days, that was a small fortune. So, in the summer of 1969, after an extended furlough in the States (allowing Dad to complete his PhD work), they would return to El Salvador, gather our belongings, and then go back up to Mexico's Yucatan peninsula to begin a new work there.

Dad had traveled there in February to explore the possibility of forming a new radio station and had been met with a welcoming response. So, on June 24, the day after Lizbeth's high school graduation, Dad, Mom, Lizbeth, David Lloyd, Mark, John, and Bruce Brumalow, a friend of David Lloyd, began the long drive south—again. Lillian and I would visit as time allowed, and Lizbeth and David Lloyd would return to the States at the end of summer. Lizbeth had been accepted at Grand View for her nurse's training, so she would begin her training just as I completed mine.

Another Long Drive South

Ready to head south again

Allowing for the typical travel annoyances, overall the trip went well, even the border crossing, where it appeared that they might hit their first real snag. Bruce didn't have a signed permission slip from his parents. But an eight-dollar gift to the border guards quickly solved that problem. Fortunately, my parents had only good intentions for Bruce. I shudder when I think how easy it would have been for kidnappers to whisk a child across that border for nefarious purposes.

After a brief break at the Presbyterian Bible Institute in Villa Hermosa, they began the final leg of their journey to the Yucatan peninsula, often driving through swarms of pesky mosquitoes and then swarms of hungry dragonflies pursuing the mosquitoes. They were grateful for the mosquito predators, but still it was unnerving when the big, bug-eyed hoverers got inside their car.

They were grateful when, upon their arrival at the Gulf coast, they got to walk across white sands to the cool, refreshing water. Farther south, as in Costa Rica, the beach sands are black.

After retracing their drive to the coast, they were back on the highway. When they arrived at the El Salvador border, they learned that war had broken out between El Salvador and Honduras. More travel difficulties were likely—in fact, the police at the crossing warned them of dangers ahead. But they really had no choice. Before long they were stopped by the first of two large crowds of machete-wielding peasants who insisted on searching their car. The people said they were looking for poisoned cookies, which their enemies had been feeding to their children. Ultimately, and with many thanks to God, my family made it back to the trailer house in El Salvador, where they could prepare for the move to Yucatan.

But first they had some last-minute repairs and upgrades to make at the station in El Salvador. They installed a new console, cataloged hundreds of records, and changed the feedline to the tower.

When all the various kids' travels settled for the start of the new school year, only Mark and John would stay in Yucatan with our parents.

Mom and Dad were no longer young parents with a brood of little children. Their kids were becoming adults and would soon be looking for their own ways to serve the Lord. Each Solt child was a unique individual, but our parents had modeled for all of us the joy of Christian service—even amid hardships.

In her Christmas letter at the end of 1969, Mom wrote the following:

We just held a communications workshop for pastors and laymen of the Reformed Church. We have many opportunities to speak and offer special music in the local churches. It is a real blessing getting to know the pastors and their people. We have been working closely with them in forming a radio board. There seems to be harmony and seeking the Lord's blessing on this new work. Plans are going ahead for a recording studio, and Neil Macaulay will be flying down some used audio equipment for it on December 12. Pray that we may get it in duty free.

A radio group has been formally organized also in the city of Villahermosa (about 450 miles south of here) and is applying for a radio station frequency. The brethren in Becal (50 miles south) have the land but no frequency as yet. Pray that soon it may be granted too.

These last few days have been occupied in writing and re-writing television scripts. We have at our disposal 21 hours of free time over the holidays on a local TV station. Pray for the impact of these programs as well as for the people who will receive the Spanish New Testament, "Good News for Modern Man," which we will be offering. This is the beginning of a distribution of 200,000 New Testaments and of 25,000 Bibles in a door-to-door visitation outreach for the whole of Yucatan. David is in charge of the promotion for this program, which means training classes, distribution and follow-up. We will be using radio and television extensively. We will appreciate your special prayers for this project in 1970.

Life in Yucatan

The week before Easter, my parents began showing the Barabbas film they had produced with Hermano Pablo back in El Salvador. In addition, they began using radio, TV, and newspaper ads and notices to publicize a

New Testament distribution campaign in the Yucatan area. Then they began the door-to-door campaign of home visits. In a letter to supporters shortly after the campaign, Mom wrote, *"It was a joy to lead one lady to the Lord."*

Shortly after that, Dad went to southwestern Mexico to help Missionary Aviation Fellowship and Wycliffe Translators with some radio work, and while there looked at the possibility of building a station that could minister to one of the largest Indian tribes in Mexico. At about that same time, Mom wrote, *"We have recently formed here in Merida the women's auxiliary of the radio work called the C.C.C. (Co-laborers with Christ). Our first prayer meeting had 27 ladies present and we felt the presence of the Lord."*

During the time of that campaign, two missionaries from the Pocket Testament League and two local Christian men lived with them and helped with the distribution. Those men had a truck equipped with a public address system, a record player, and floodlights; attracting curious crowds wasn't difficult. Mom wrote that in one town they quickly attracted a crowd that they estimated to be nearly 500, and they had no trouble distributing all 400 of their Testaments. Each of the Testaments had a response slip inside for those who would want to follow up through correspondence. Nearly 200 returned the slips. Through Mom's letters I could almost hear her joyous enthusiasm at God's wonderful works of grace.

All that was just the preparation stage for the real campaign, when Hermano Pablo preached to more than 30,000 adults and 3,000 children at a local soccer stadium over the course of several days.

Meanwhile, back in the States, I was getting just a bit nervous about taking my State Board nursing exams, not because I feared failing them, but because I was having a tough time convincing the officials that I really was an American citizen. Thank God, it all worked out.

John Learns a Painful Lesson

Near the end of 1970, Mexico had just elected a new president, and the schools had given the students the day off for the inauguration. Ten-year-old John and several of his friends were celebrating with the same enthusiasm—and the same method—as many of their Mexican

108

neighbors, by shooting off fireworks. John's pockets were full of them when one he lit somehow managed to explode too close; it set off the firecrackers in his pockets. His pants lit on fire, and you can guess which parts of his anatomy were burned most severely.

Mom, who had repeatedly warned him about the potential dangers of playing with fireworks, was at a women's ministry convention in Guatemala, so Dad rushed him to the nearby Presbyterian medical clinic. The doctors gave him a general anesthetic and then

John shows off his burns.

scrubbed his burned skin for an hour before they could treat it. He had to spend the following two days at the clinic for observation and further treatments. When Mom returned, he was afraid to face her as he recalled her many warnings. When she entered his room, he said, simply, "Mommy, I learned the hard way."

Lois and Doug; Libet and Bruce

I met Douglas Robert Emr at Philadelphia College of the Bible (now PBU). I was his secretary in the student missionary union, and after a year of working together, he proposed to me in December 1970. He was in the pastoral studies program, and I was in the Bible program after my nursing studies so

Doug and I were married July 3, 1971.

that I could be a missionary nurse. It took a lot of praying to accept his proposal. We took a trip to Mexico so he could me my parents. I don't know that they were 100 percent for him, but they knew I loved him, so they gave me their blessings.

They came to our wedding, July 3, 1971, at Bethany Bible Fellowship Church, in Hatfield, Pennsylvania. Pastor Ron Mahurin married us. The church provided a garden reception with flowers all around, beautiful cake, and finger foods. We honeymooned in Canada, at Horace Holt's cabin near Niagara Falls.

Less than half a year later, on December 16, 1971, Lisbeth married Bruce Detweiler—in the same Pennsylvania church and presided over by the same pastor, Ron Mahurin.

Lizbet and Bruce were married December 16, 1971.

Furlough and Back Again, 1972
Dad, Mom, Mark, and John spent much of 1972 living in a beautiful country home near Telford, Pennsylvania, while on another furlough in the States. Meanwhile, Doug and I were living in an apartment, but were planning to move in with Dad and Mom for a month while we did some work for the home church there. Lillian was nearing the completion of her studies at Philadelphia College of the Bible and had applied to work with Latin American Mission following her graduation. Lizbeth was preparing to take her state boards to become a registered nurse, and David Lloyd was working on his undergrad degree in electrical engineering at Syracuse University. As the year wound down, my parents were eager to return to their ministry in Mexico, but Mom's health wasn't at its best.

Not What They Planned

Latin American Evangelist magazine ran this article about my parents in 1972.

A feature article in the November/December 1972 Latin American Evangelist magazine gave an accurate account of my parents' ministry in Yucatan. It noted that because of a long governmental delay in getting a license for the radio station, Dad and Mom simply followed the Spirit's leading and improvised in order to continue the Lord's work there.

With evangelical Christians making up just two percent of the area's population, my parents had no shortage of opportunities. They simply packed their car full of films and equipment and drove across the flat, harsh Yucatan plains, from village to village. They ran the evangelistic films more than 1,000 times to audiences totaling more than 150,000 people—and 6,000 of those attendees confessed Christ as their Savior.

The article stated,

> At one small town of 250 people, everyone attended the meeting, and—they all came forward when the invitation was given. Dave says, "My first reaction was that they didn't understand what they were doing." But they did. Of the 250, fifty have been baptized already, and they are working to win their neighbors in the next town to Christ.

Considering that both of them also taught at two local seminaries (one Baptist and one Presbyterian), I'd have to say that God gave my parents a busy and fruitful ministry.

Mom taught several courses, including homiletics (preaching).

Dad also taught many courses, including media courses, which included instruction in the use of projectors.

Chapter Sixteen

A Heartbreaking Loss Amid God's Wondrous Works

ೞ

Doug and I joined Africa Inland Mission (AIM) in 1973. We went to Newark, New Jersey, to work with African-Americans in a new home-front endeavor since we were not approved to go across the seas to Africa. I was pregnant with our first boy. We were having difficulty finding out what our salary should be so that we could communicate with our supporters. Our director was a theorist and Doug was a pragmatist. Having lived in the rough neighborhoods of North Philadelphia for six years, Doug was good with gangs and reaching out to the African-American pastors; he helped in the inner city Sunday schools. Finally we came to an impasse and we amicably parted company with AIM and returned to Souderton, Pennsylvania, in December 1973. Harold Detweiler provided us a house rent free. By then I was eight months pregnant. This house had a wallpapered baby room, so my family put gifts from four showers in the room. They were helping us move in and I just sat and directed. Little did I know that a month later, in January 1974, I would return to that house with empty arms—no baby—to face a room filled lovingly with gifts from friends and family. My heart was broken; my parents had left just a month before—so far away, in Mexico. God healed our hearts, and I still love my Lord and know that these difficult lessons have taken off some of the rough edges of my life.

Matthew Emr

Dad, Mom, Mark, and John returned to Mexico after Christmas. On January 27, 1974, I went into labor and my mother was far away. Doug was there to encourage me at Grand View Hospital. Early in the labor the nurses could not get a fetal heartbeat, but they didn't tell me. Doug knew this and called our pastor, Ron Mahurin, to come to the hospital. My labor grew stronger, but they gave me no pain medicine because the doctor couldn't hear the fetal heartbeat. On January 28, Matthew Emr was stillborn. How I wished my mother was close by. I called her from the hospital and talked with her in far away in Mexico. Of course we both were distraught.

The following day, Dad wrote this to me:

> *How saddened we were to hear the news of your baby. So much has happened to you, which all seems to be against you, but our God never makes a mistake. How wonderful to know that way back at Christmas God was already preparing the way for you to be near your family and friends. This is special comfort to us. We trust that this experience will not make any of us bitter, but submissive to the holy will of God, our Heavenly Father, who loves us and is still on the throne.*

That was an especially difficult time for Doug and me, not just because of the loss of our baby, but also because our entire future took a dramatic and, at the time, perplexing turn.

David Lloyd's Wedding

David and Patricia Friday were married June 14, 1975, at Emmanuel Lutheran Church in New Brunswick, New Jersey. The reception was held in Pat's back yard, in North Brunswick, under a big tent. Family and friends enjoyed lots of good Hungarian food and fellowship!

David and Pat are married.

Mark's Soccer Skills

Soccer is immensely popular in Mexico and Latin America, so it was no surprise that Mark, who'd lived more of his life in Latin American countries than in the States, became enamored with the game. They say that practice makes perfect, and playing as often as he did made Mark, if not quite Pele, an immensely talented player. So when he returned to the States to finish high school, his skills quickly impressed coaches, fans, and sports writers.

The newspaper article about Mark included a picture of him and some of his soccer awards.

He lived with the Hawkins and Jenkins families in Souderton, Pennsylvania, and soon became the local high school's star player. He captured several scoring titles and won many awards, even being selected for the all-state team. But we Solts were proudest of him for his Christian testimony. In 1975, during his senior year, he told a reporter,

"If I'm destined to continue in soccer, someone will discover me and I'll get my break. If not, I'll have solid Bible training [from Philadelphia Bible College] *and I can go on to missionary work or whatever God wants me to do."*

A Busy Family

Mom and Dad were planning a two-month stay in the States, from April 15 to June 15, in order to attend many events with their now mostly grown children. They planned to be present for the birth of the new baby Doug and I were expecting; for David Lloyd's graduation from graduate school at Syracuse University, and then his wedding; Mark's high school graduation; and John's completion of training for his ham radio license.

Meanwhile, along with their busy daily routine, Dad and Mom also were part of the committee responsible for preparing for Dr. Luis Palau and his evangelistic team to come and speak at a statewide evangelistic campaign in 1976. At that time Dr. Palau was an up-and-coming evangelist who had modeled his ministry along the lines of Billy

Graham's crusades. In fact, Dr. Palau had at one time worked for Dr. Graham.

When Dr. Palau came to the area to begin the pre-campaign preparations, Dad was the one to meet him at the airport and drive him to the camp where the planning would begin.

In their 1975 Christmas letter to supporters, my parents wrote,

March '76 is fast approaching for the statewide evangelistic campaign with Luis Palau, and David as advisor to the local committee. Many preparations and much training must yet be done, but we do praise the Lord that we have been given the bullfight ring at a very reasonable price. It was an answer to prayer, since it was denied us for a campaign several years ago. There are special meetings for young people, women and professionals each month. This past week, children's counselors were trained with the hopes that these would continue to hold weekly children's clubs year 'round. We know you will praise the Lord for His goodness in answering prayer. Keep praying that many will come to know the Lord through Luis Palau's radio and TV programs that are nowbeing aired.

Mom later reported that 5,000 people signed cards of interest at the Palau campaign. Plenty of follow-up was called for—as soon as they returned from a trip to the States.

Back for the Bicentennial

Dad, Mom, and John made it back to the States for the late spring and summer of 1976, just as the nation was preparing to celebrate its official 200th birthday. Happily for all, their return also coincided with the arrival of their first grandson, Jonathan Bruce Detweiler, Liz and her husband Bruce's baby. (After our loss of Matthew, Doug and I were blessed with the birth of our daughter Joy, on May 9, 1975. Joy was Mom and Dad's first grandchild.)

Their trip also allowed Mom and Dad to host a DiValentino family reunion in Philadelphia, which, not surprisingly, was the center of the nation's bicentennial celebration.

Thirty Years as Missionaries

Nineteen seventy seven marked the thirty-year anniversary of my parents' beginning as Latin American missionaries, and what a time they'd had serving the Lord.

In 1976 alone they'd presented the gospel to more than 184,000 people via films and television, and they'd seen 3,000 people come to know Jesus as their Savior as a result of those presentations. But even more amazing is that in just the first eight months of 1977 they'd already seen those 1976 totals surpassed. One day in glory, I expect to see a long line of people thanking my parents for introducing them to their Savior and Lord.

Mom and Dad were still happy after 30 years as missionaries.

Dad and Mom also praised the Lord that in 1977—seven years after applying for their station frequency—the license finally was awarded. However, by that time, some of the equipment was outdated or no longer serviceable. They also continued to teach at the local seminaries, and to prepare for and work at summer camps.

Off to Europe—Then Back Home to Blessings

In 1978 my parents spent two months in Europe—in eleven countries—helping Mark and John as summer missionaries, and working with seven different mission boards. They also got to spend some time with Lillian, who at the time was living in England and studying midwife nursing. Mom was especially thrilled to meet many DiValentino relatives in Italy.

Even then, in the late 70s, most Europeans had become products of their post-Christian culture. Dad and Mom found the general European apathy toward spiritual things in general and evangelical Christianity specifically discouraging. They returned to Mexico with heavy hearts over that European apathy—and with a renewed appreciation for their Mexican neighbors' openness to the gospel.

Later that year, Thanksgiving Day for Americans, my parents held final exams for their students at the Baptist seminary. Around the same time, they also participated in another Luis Palau campaign, this time in Acapulco. In their Christmas letter to supporters, they wrote,

> *The campaign with Luis Palau in Acapulco was a real success, in spite of much opposition from Communist sources. Besides the evening meetings in the baseball stadium, where more than 5,000 attended each night, there were teas, banquets, and meetings for special groups. Altogether, more than 2,000 made decisions. The first night, unknown to each other, a husband and wife who had been separated for many months, each came forward from opposite sides of the stadium to receive the Lord. They not only received the Lord, but saw each other, became reconciled, and went home together!*

Closing out the 70s

As the 70s drew to a close, my parents, by then in their late 50s were still going strong, ministering for the Lord who had called them into His service more than thirty years before. They continued to distribute Bibles and biblical literature, as well as show Christian films, and teach at the seminary. The radio station for Yucatan was, however, still on hold. The work continued, but, as they wrote in their 1979 Christmas letter, *"It just seems that there is one thing after another that holds up their* [necessary parts] *arrival."*

Mom taught an extension class in Campeche, Mexico.

But a family reunion was in the offing, as they wrote in that same Christmas letter:

> *On December 10ᵗʰ, between seminary semesters, we will be taking Mark with us to the States. We'll pick up John in Texas and head for Pennsylvania to spend Christmas with the family (everyone except Lillian). Join us in praying for good weather and for safety while traveling. We hope to be back here January 4ᵗʰ. We look forward to being with the family as Elizabeth, Bruce, and Joshua were all in the hospital at the same time with some bug they caught down here while visiting us. We are thankful that Jonathan did not get sick. We know that many of you were praying and so we are grateful to each of you, and of course to the Lord for His goodness in healing them.*

Chapter Seventeen

Praise the Lord—Gospel Radio for Yucatan!

❧

Finally, in 1980, after more than a decade of prayers, hard work, and seemingly endless delays, the Yucatan radio station was on the air! In their April 16, 1980, support letter, my parents wrote this:

> *"Sing praises to God, sing praises; Sing praises to our King, sing praises for God is the King of all the earth.... Great is the Lord and greatly to be praised" (Psalm 47:6, 7; 48:11). WE ARE ON THE AIR for about four hours a day with what we call "test broadcasts" giving testimony that JESUS SAVES!*

Although, because of some government restrictions, at the time they were able to broadcast only in very short segments (no more than five minutes), they already were hearing reports of people listening to the programs from as far away as 100 miles. At that point, they were just waiting for the government inspection and approval. The people in the nearby village were thrilled to have a radio station right next door.

Meanwhile, Grandpa Solt was visiting them again and was helping them as they traveled the area, showing *The Cross and The Switchblade* movie about the life and salvation of former gang leader Nicky Cruz. In addition, they were planning for an even bigger event: Nicky Cruz was scheduled to come to the Merida area for a series of rallies in August.

Later in 1980, Mom asked for prayer for Rock, a man she met outside one of the theaters where they were showing evangelistic films. Rock, a former bullfighter, was willing to talk—and listen to the gospel

118

message—but apparently he was on drugs and not fully coherent. She wrote that *"his life seems to be wasting away."* She also asked for prayer for Victor, a young man they'd met under similar circumstances and who, because of various disappointments, had turned to liquor rather than to the Lord.

God's Special Favor?

Also in 1980, Mom reported that a letter sent to other Mexican radio stations prohibiting the broadcast of any religious programs never arrived at their station, so they continued their broadcasts. They could only guess why the letter made its way to other Mexican radio stations—many of which had to cancel their religious broadcasts—but not to theirs. They asked for prayer for the other stations, but meanwhile they praised the Lord that their work could continue. While the broadcasts continued, so did the additions to the station, including a reception room and a recording studio.

By that time, the two youngest Solt kids were also following Dad and Mom in serving the Lord. Mark was a Dallas Theological Seminary student, and John was in his second year at LeTourneau University, learning to become a missionary aviator.

1981: Another Busy Year

My parents discovered the town of Solt, in Hungary.

In March of 1981 the Yucatan station celebrated one year of broadcasting. Later in the year, most of us were able to take a brief break from our various ministries and business dealings and reunite before heading off again in many directions. Mom and Dad would return to El Salvador in August for the dedication of the new radio station there. Then, in September, they would leave for a three-month stay in Germany, where they would help with radio and TV ministries directed toward Eastern Europe.

A fun and exciting twist on the Solt trip to Europe was discovering the town of Solt in Hungary, about fifty miles south of Budapest. It seems that the passport clerks there were excited to meet some real American Solts.

Late in 1981, after their return from Europe, in a letter to supporters, Dad wrote of the persecution in communist countries:

The radio survey in Yugoslavia, Rumania and Hungary confirmed the fact that something must be done locally by medium wave instead of short wave if we are to reach the people behind the iron curtain. Radio seems to be the only way to get through to evangelize the unsaved and encourage those who already know the Lord but are held in slavery in many different ways.

He also reported that *"We will be returning to Europe for about eight months on March 15 to make a more permanent installation. Doors are opening in other countries as well, so keep praying as we meet the challenge."*

Shortly after their return, they were eagerly anticipating (as were the rest of us) the family gathering in Merced, California, for Mark's December 18 wedding with Colleen Hadley. Less than two months after Mark's wedding, Doug and I welcomed our fourth child into our family. Daniel was born February 4, 1982.

Back in Mexico—Briefly

After Dad and Mom returned to Mexico, they compiled the 1981 film report. They had completed 4,986 showings to audiences totaling 611,853 people; and 4,614 of those who viewed the films, made decisions to trust Christ as their Savior. Then, during the 1982 Mardi Gras season, while Mom and Grandpa Solt (still going strong at 85) continued the film ministry in Mexico, Dad returned to help again in El Salvador. He wrote, *"The heart cry of the believers was: 'Tell the U.S. to send help, otherwise we will be overtaken by the guerrillas and communists.'"*

Intercontinental Spiritual Warriors

By this point, my parents were in their 60s and, despite the aches and pains that accompany the aging process, they were still periodically crossing the ocean to minister on two different continents. Because of the global ministry God gave them—as they worked to get the gospel to Eastern Europeans who already had fallen under the reign of godless communism and to El Salvadorians who feared the encroachment of brutal communist guerillas—they had an up-front view of the frontlines of that era's most potent spiritual battles. They might not have been able to see the spirits wrestling in the heavenlies, but they could see the results of those battles right here on earth.

In one letter, after a trip into several communist-controlled Eastern European countries, Dad wrote,

> We came back with very heavy hearts for the believers over there. We had to meet one pastor in a park because his home is being watched 24 hours a day. His home is bugged (hidden microphones to hear all that is said) and in August he was interrogated four times; some of the things they questioned him about were private, so he realized even his home was not safe. He has been jailed four different times for his faith!

Then, after returning to Mexico, Dad had to take a quick trip to help out in El Salvador. But the night he arrived there, communist agitators blew up the local sugar mill and two radio stations. They also burned several buses and torched a sugar cane field. Not surprisingly, then, he had to cancel part of his trip. But he reported that, despite all the communist-inspired mayhem—or perhaps in reaction to it—people there were packing the churches and turning to the Lord.

It was at about that same time, late spring 1983, that Mark was ordained at Scofield Memorial Church and then officially graduated from Dallas Theological Seminary the following day. Then, the following week, John graduated from LeTourneau College, having completed a double major in aviation and electrical technology. The Solts missionary legacy was firmly established.

Shortly after that, LAM headquarters told Dad and Mom it was time for them to take another furlough, so they spent the first two months of their furlough back in Europe, where they'd seen such a great need amid the post-Christian culture and the dark oppression of communist control. Imagine, even in their mid sixties, and after more than thirty years in missions service, they still spent much of their free time serving the Lord.

While in Germany, Dad put his many technical and handyman skills to good use, repairing recorders, copiers, and other electrical devices for missionaries there.

They also spent some of that furlough time in Mom's ancestral home, Italy. Of that trip, Mom wrote,

> *Our dream of seeing an AM radio station on the air* [in Italy] *has dissolved into a vapor. We are very disappointed but we must accept this as the will of the Lord at this time. The Italian blood in me still cries out for the salvation of my people. The Lord is blessing the church planting ministry in northern Italy. Pray that many will be converted and make Him Lord of their lives.*

Back in Mexico—1984

Dad enjoyed training young pastors.

Not long after returning to Merida, Dad and Mom were again fully involved in evangelism. This time they helped with a campaign held at the Poliforum Stadium. The scheduled evangelist couldn't make it, but Dad's old friend Elmer Bueno, another evangelist filled in and, along with the films my parents showed, gave the attendees some soul-piercing messages; more than 100 came forward to call on Jesus as their Savior. Mom and Dad continued helping with evangelism, visitations, station maintenance, and teaching at the Baptist seminary, which in the autumn of that year closed, but then re-opened as a Bible institute.

As 1984 wound to a close, Dad and Mom reported that classes at the re-opened Bible institute were going well and that they also were keeping busy by helping the local chapter of Gideons International. They wrote that at one of the jails where Gideons distributed New Testaments, all the inmates were under age fifteen—highlighting the great need for the continued work to present the gospel.

Nicaragua Update

In 1986 Dad flew to our old home city of San Jose, Costa Rica, and from there drove to one of our other old hometowns, Managua, Nicaragua, to offer some advice and help for those carrying on the gospel work there. He reported that Rolando Mena, the station manager was optimistic about their work there despite the fact that *"the night before the main power transformer of the 15 kw AM transmitter burned out."* He added this:

> They were able to find a replacement in Nicaragua, however the cost is over one thousand dollars. This is quite a sum to raise when the daily minimum wage of Nicaraguans is between 30 and 40 cents (US).

Dad also wrote about Asociacion Cultural Nicaraguense, the non-denominational board, made up of leaders from local Nazarene, Baptist, and Pentecostal churches.

Dad concluded,

> The transmitter, which I built 27 years ago, definitely needs replacement. In consultation with Robert Remington and Hugh Worsfold (engineers who have both helped ONDAS DE LUZ in the past) we decided that the best plan would be to purchase a new 12 kw AM transmitter manufactured by ELCOR here in Costa Rica.
>
> This is a first-class product with state of the art circuitry. The price including an audio limiter and tower tuning unit will be about $48,000 (US). This is a better price than we could get anywhere else, and in addition shipping costs will be less and replacement parts easily accessible.

Lillian—in Costa Rica

On July 22, 1987, Lillian gave Mom and Dad their twelfth grandchild, Lillian Rebeca Ramirez, who would henceforth be addressed simply as Rebeca. But little Rebeca's entrance into this world was not easy. We thanked God that Lillian was able to give birth in La Clinica Biblica, with her own doctor attending. After complications with an attempt to induce labor, the doctor determined that a C-section was necessary. But that procedure also had complications. A week or so after the birth, Lillian wrote the following:

123

It was decided I should have an epidural anesthesia to bring my blood pressure down, and that way I would also be awake when Rebeca was born. Due to my unstable high blood pressure and other factors, I reacted violently to the anesthesia. My blood pressure dropped so low that I went into shock and started to convulse and vomit before they could get it under control. I guess I gave everyone in the operating room quite a scare before they got me stabilized. Fabi, my former roommate and who many of you know, was with me the whole time and was a great encouragement. Praise the Lord, many of you were praying at this time as all I recall was, "I am going to die!"

Praise God, Lillian didn't die! Both she and Rebeca came through okay. Her letter added, *"Rebeca was born 12:30 A.M., and all I remember was the crying and seeing her head full of long, black hair. Rebeca is the most beautiful baby I have ever seen!"*

Mom went to San Jose to visit Lillian and Rebeca, and then, as she pondered Jose's abandonment of Lillian, she wrote this to Dad:

You are very special to me. ... I could see our life bonded together in more ways than one. Our six children have helped, but even before that I pledged you my heart and life that wherever the Lord led you, I would be willing to follow because you were all that I wanted—to be with you was sufficient. We have been through many heartaches together, but you have been an inspiration to me and a help. I don't think I would have survived it alone, as Lillian is doing.

Forty Years in Missions Work

In the Bible, the number forty often refers to a time of testing or trials. The rains during the flood of Noah's time lasted forty days. Moses spent forty years of testing in the desert before the exodus. The children of Israel then wandered in the desert for forty years of testing. After Jesus had fasted for forty days, Satan tempted him in the wilderness.

I am happy to write that, after forty years of serving the Lord in bringing His gospel to the nations, my parents had proved faithful, to each other and their children, but most especially to their calling as missionaries. They are not perfect, and we were not the perfect family, but clearly my parents loved their Lord, and their love for Him inspired every one of their children to become involved, in one way or another, in taking the gospel to the lost and in serving Jesus. In a letter dated right about the time of their forty-year anniversary of entry into missions work, Dad wrote this:

> *Many times we wonder if our film ministry produces fruit. We asked at a recent film showing, "How long has this church been here?" The pastor replied, "Don't you remember? Two years ago you showed films down at the street corner? That got the church started!" Another wonderful answer to prayer: "Jack" is the owner of a famous shirt factory here in Merida. Several years ago we showed a film in his beautiful home. He accepted the Lord some time later. This past week he took me to a church to show a film for him. After the film showing, he taught the evangelism class. He loves the Lord, and is growing in his knowledge of Him. Praise the Lord with us!*

Many families in Campeche gathered to watch gospel films in a church.

Statistics can provide a good measurement of the success of a ministry, but, sometimes, a few stories like those really put a work into clear perspective.

That's not to say that numbers are unimportant; the following year, 1988, Mom and Dad helped with another Luis Palau campaign, this time in Ciudad Victoria, followed by one in Tuxtla Gutierrez. Between the two efforts, they saw more than 5,500 people call on the Lord for salvation!

Dad worked closely with Dr. Palau.

Hurricane Gilbert

Missionaries have to accept trials along with the triumphs. On September 9, 1988, they got the joyous news that Mark and Colleen had given birth to Timothy Charles. But just a few days later, as residents of Yucatan, they endured the devastation of Hurricane Gilbert. Whole towns along the coast were obliterated. Mom and Dad were unharmed, but they grieved over the losses that many of their neighbors suffered. A lot of recovery work lay ahead.

Chapter Eighteen

The Early Nineties—Retirement Looms, Their Legacy Blooms

CR

A long with the arrival of a new decade came a new technology that would greatly affect my parents' ministry in Latin America. Videos were overtaking 16-mm films and projectors. Dad and Mom, by this point in their mid 60s, would have to adapt; and, as they'd done many times before, that's exactly what they did. Meanwhile, their teaching at the seminaries was winding down, as many of the students they'd taught decades before were now stepping into the role of professor. It was becoming clear that the time for retirement was approaching—but it hadn't arrived yet. They'd planned to retire in 1991, as they'd both passed their sixty-fifth birthday, but the mission board asked them to stay on five more years. So, after enjoying another furlough that provided a lot of time with family, they were back at work in Yucatan.

Natural Disasters and Personal Loss

As Dad and Mom continued their work in Yucatan, Lillian, raising Rebeca alone, carried on with her ministry to the people of Costa Rica, where, in April of 1991, a 7.6 magnitude earthquake killed forty-seven people and left thousands homeless. Lillian wrote,

What a disaster this earthquake has been! I've helped in five major disasters, and it seems like setting up the volunteers and work to be done is so easy, but the heartache and grief I feel for these people doesn't get easier—it's harder each time. Some nights as I lay awake (it continues to shake, 600 tremors over 3.0 on the R scale in 24 hours), trying to get some much needed sleep, I cry myself to sleep as I remember the vivid pictures of what I have just seen in Limon.

Lillian was chosen to be the medical coordinator for the Evangelical Alliance of Costa Rica, and besides all her hands-on medical work and coordination of other personnel, she needed to raise more than $13,000 for the relief work. That was a quite a responsibility for a young, single mother. She proved to be up to the task, thanks largely, I think, to the tremendous work ethic she learned from our parents.

Then, just two months later, in June 1992, the office that Lillian and her ministry rented in San Jose caught fire and, between the fire, smoke, and water damage, was virtually a total loss. Then, another two months after the office fire, much of Costa Rica was hit by torrential rains and flooding. The local paper reported,

Nature added insult to injury to Costa Rica's Atlantic Coast with a three-day deluge this week that required the emergency evacuation of 4,500 to 5,000 people throughout the region, left thousands more homeless, and caused still-untold damage to the region's banana industry, which was already reeling from last April's earthquake. Three people were reported missing in the disaster.

But for us, an even bigger heartache was sandwiched between the

April earthquake and the June fire. In May of that year Grandpa Solt died. Oh, we all knew, without any doubt, that he'd gone home to be with his Savior and Lord, Jesus. And we knew we'd see him again when our turns came to pass on to glory, but until then, we'd miss him.

Grandpa Solt posed with Uncle Paul in Aunt Myrt in 1988.

128

The Bible in Mayan

Despite their report in of their 1992 letters to supporters that, like their old pickup truck, their old bodies were wearing out, my parents continued their ministry in Yucatan. And in that same year, 1992, they had the pleasure of reporting that the translation of the Bible into Mayan had been completed. They wrote,

> On November 6, the Mayan Bible, which was in translation for ten years and published by the Bible Society of Mexico, was dedicated and presented to the Mayan people. The theater was packed and a special edition was presented to the governor of Yucatan, Dulce Ma Sauri Riancho. She gave a very appreciative speech. All the evangelical denominations were present to witness this exciting event.

Shortly after that they were invited to the dedication of a new church in Cancun. When they arrived, they were overjoyed to discover that the special speaker for the event was a pastor who had been one of their students at the seminary nearly two decades before. Doug and I would have been excited to be there rejoicing with them, but we were on a mission trip to Ukraine.

A Special Anniversary

In July of 1993 my parents were invited to the forty-fifth anniversary celebration for radio station TIFC in San Jose, Costa Rica, the station they'd help establish—the second oldest missionary radio station in the world. What a reunion it was. The young law student who had been one of their on-air announcers, way back at the beginning, had gone on to become a justice on Costa Rica's Supreme Court. By the time of the reunion, he'd retired—a fact not lost on my parents, who were nearly seventy. But God wasn't finished with their ministry—not quite yet.

When TIFC was founded, the station was built on open land, surrounded by coffee plantations, but in the ensuing forty-five years the area had become urbanized. It was time to build a new station. In just one week, LAM was able to raise $80,000 to purchase new land some ten miles from the original station. My parents reported this good news:

> Some testified that they had asked the Lord only for a property, but the Lord gave them not only the land, but a big beautiful house

in which they can accommodate 32 persons for retreats. The one AM transmitter and tower are already installed at the new site. They will not lose any air time as they will move each of the four transmitters one at a time. They have repeater stations in different parts of Costa Rica so they are really covering the whole country.

While they were in Costa Rica, Mom and Dad also had the joy of visiting Lillian and Rebeca. In the same report of their time at the TIFC anniversary and their reunion with Lillian, they also were able to report that the nineteen-bed hospital back in Yucatan had been completed and dedicated in May.

More of My Parents' Legacy

The apostle Paul wrote to the church in Ephesus that God "gave some *as* apostles, and some *as* prophets, and some *as* evangelists, and some *as* pastors and teachers, for the equipping of the saints for the work of service, to the building up of the body of Christ" (Ephesians 4:11-12). I truly believe that God gave my parents as "gifts" (see Ephesians 4:8) to the people of Latin America. I say that not in a boastful or arrogant manner, but simply as what I believe is a clear fulfillment of Scripture. Among God's greatest gifts to people are other people whom He uses (as prophets, evangelists, pastors, and teachers) to present the great truths of His Word. I think it's abundantly clear that God used Dad and Mom in several of these roles. The key outcome in their fulfilling those roles is seen in "the building up of the body of Christ." Luis Castillo is a good example of this "building" ministry.

On Sunday, May 29, 1994, my parents were present as the congregation of "Region 101" laid the cornerstone for the construction of a new church building. Luis Castillo, who had been my parents' interpreter long before, was the pastor of this growing congregation. My parents wrote,

> Our work teams have done house-to-house visitation and ministered with special programs. We praise the Lord that they have all the permits to begin construction; however, the first phase of the construction must be finished within six months.

Sadly, not all who proclaim to be followers of the Lord behave in a manner that glorifies Him. In that same support letter, my parents added,

The love of money causes people in positions of authority to yield to temptation and claim some of it as their own, as has happened with our manager. She was the widow of our first manager at the radio station.

Also in that letter, Mom and Dad asked for prayer for Doug and me as we were about to leave for full-time service in Ukraine; for our daughter Joy, who was about to begin nursing school; and for Liz and Bruce's son Jonathan, as he was about to leave home to be a student at Eastern Mennonite College. Clearly, David and Georgina Solt's legacy had become strong and vast—thanks to God.

Mom was struggling with a torn tendon in her foot, along with some other ailments, but she didn't let mere physical problems stop her. In their December 1995 support letter Dad wrote this:

Praise the Lord for all the work that was accomplished by the work teams in January and March. We were able to put a concrete roof on a church in the outskirts of Cancun. The members are slowly working on it and have the inside plastered and painted as well as a platform built. Thanks for your prayers. Georgina just held a Christian education workshop for 12 members of this same church. Pray that they will put into practice what they have learned.

He added that, in 1994, they held 5,149 film showings viewed by more than a quarter million precious souls, and 2,014 of them chose to become Christ followers.

Yucatan Hurricanes

On September 30, 1995, my parents, along with their Yucatan neighbors, endured the winds and floodwaters of Hurricane Opal, which killed fifty Mexicans before it veered east across the Gulf of Mexico and toward Florida's west coast. The storm-surge reached right up to my parents' home, but stopped just short of entering and causing damage. Then, less than two weeks later, on October 10, Hurricane Roxanne hit, causing still more damage, mostly from flooding. It was a rough year for the people of the Yucatan coast. Mom wrote, *"We just finished an evangelistic campaign with emphasis on 'The Crisis' here and encouraging families to trust in the Lord. There was good response."*

Solt Family Update

On June 4, 1996, Dad and Mom were back in Pennsylvania to renew their visas, for medical treatments, and to get reacquainted with old friends. Their letter gave a good update of the entire family, so I have copied it here:

> *Dear Friends,*
>
> *As I sit here in the beautiful woods of Pennsylvania, I am reminded of God's faithfulness in His marvelous creation, "The heavens declare the glory of God; and the firmament sheweth His handiwork" (Ps. 19:1).*
>
> *The full moon looks the same here as in Mexico. We are in the States to renew our six-month visas, attend Georgina's 55th high school reunion, David's 50th Swarthmore College reunion, and a number of family reunions, graduation from high school for two grandsons; for Lois and Doug's 25th anniversary, our 50th anniversary, checkups for Georgina's tendonitis, and David's six-month appointment for his damaged retina. Pray with us for complete healing.*
>
> *Lois and Doug are home from Ukraine for three months. The Lord has provided a beautifully furnished five-bedroom home so they can have their four children living with them. A wonderful answer to prayer. Joy is in her third year at Pensacola Christian College and Douglas will be joining her. He graduated with honors last night. Dave and Dan are readjusting well to the USA.*
>
> *Lillian and Rebeca from Costa Rica will be in the States for five weeks of deputation. Rebeca helps speak also to help raise support so they can return fully supported.*
>
> *Liz and Bruce have offered their home to each member of our family. We all like to consider them our Home Office Base as they care for each of us. "As his part is that goeth down to the battle, so—shall his part be that tarrieth by the stuff, they shall part alike" (1 Samuel 30:24). Their kindness and hospitality have blessed many of us. Son Joshua graduates this week and will be going to Philadelphia College of the Bible. Jon continues at Hahnemann. Andrew's a live wire who likes to imitate his brothers.*

132

Dave and Pat are in Singapore at the time of this writing, promoting their solid state transmitters at a trade show. Dave has designed a 500-watt transistorized transmitter that fits in a suitcase. Ben, Susana, Paul and Laura are staying with friends this week.

Mark and Ruth Colleen are pastoring a Spanish church in Newark, N. J. He is discipling Lorenzo to be the full-time pastor and sells Prudential insurance to support his family. Karisa, Dan and Tim are being home-schooled. Caleb and Joshua are in kindergarten nearby.

John and Lisa work with Dave at the transmitter factory, trying to keep up with traveling to different places to iron out any transmitter problems as well as teaching a men's Bible Study. Lisa is active at home with Philip, Matthew, and Alyssa as well as in the primary department as SS superintendent.

As we look forward to our 50th anniversary, we are praising the Lord for His goodness over the years of serving him in Latin America. He has supplied all our needs far above what we anticipated. Praise Him with us. The enclosed is a personal invitation to our 50th wedding anniversary. We hope you will come so we can personally thank you for your partnership with us over these many years. Since we have been spending more time in Cancun, we have changed our postal address to: Apartado 975, Cancun, Q.R., 77501 Mexico.

We will be returning July 24, continuing to live in the same apartment and will be repairing projectors, films, and videos as well as anything else the Lord calls us to do. We plan to officially retire June 30, 1997, but will continue with all our ministries in Mexico. We are in the midst of training a young Mexican to carry on the film office in Merida. Pray that he will be faithful. Again our special thanks for being a part of our team. Continue to pray for each of us. GOD BLESS YOU RICHLY.

Gratefully in Him,
David and Georgina

Chapter Nineteen

Retirement—They Have "Finished the Race"

CR

David and Georgina Solt officially retired on September 27, 1997, exactly fifty years after their Latin American Missions ministry began. The LAM offices were the sight of a grand farewell banquet for Dad, Mom, and six other longtime LAM missionaries who also had retired recently. I wish I could have attended.

Although my parents retired "officially" in late September 1997, they couldn't just shut down. God's work is never finished. So when Mom, Liz, and I flew to San Jose, Costa Rica, in 1998, to visit Lillian and to celebrate Mom's seventy-fifth birthday, we all pitched in to help Lillian with relief efforts in nearby Nicaragua in the wake of Hurricane Mitch. It was a wonderful time of ministry and of just enjoying being together.

But, like all good things, the reunion had to end. Liz and I returned to our husbands, in the States, and Mom returned to Dad, in Cancun— hey, they had officially retired, but why leave the land that had become their home, at least while their health allowed them to stay. Mom did have a scare, though, when she found a lump in her breast, but it was removed and it turned out to be a non-malignant cyst. Even in their seventies, my parents still enjoyed a five-mile ride on their tandem bike every morning.

Despite their "official" retirement, my parents still often answered calls for help. Mom reported on teaching another homiletics (preaching) class, and Dad still answered calls to help with technical issues at the radio station. Serving others had been at the center of their life together, they couldn't just stop "cold turkey."

Back to the States for Dad's Back

While Mom and Dad enjoyed helping out through their retirement in Cancun, by late 1999 it was becoming clear that Dad's worsening sciatica was becoming too much; they'd have to return to the States for medical treatment. Mom wrote,

> David has been experiencing sciatic pain for over a year and the pain is getting worse, so we have decided to go to the States to be checked by our doctor up there. Any projects he undertakes are very difficult as he cannot stand for long or walk. We shall appreciate your prayers for healing. We will be flying to the States on December 8 and returning January 11.

After four treatments and a lot of prayers, Dad got the relief he'd been hoping for. In their November 2000 letter to friends and supporters, my parents wrote,

> As we look over the past year, our hearts are full of thanksgiving and praise to God for the miracle He has done in David's life. He suffered with much pain down both legs due to stenosis of the spine. He was unable to stand or walk for over a year. After four different stays in Grand View Hospital in Sellersville, PA, God answered your prayers, our Mexican friends' prayers and ours! It really is a miracle as David has had no pain since! He is able to carry on repairing films and projectors.

At that point, some might have thought it prudent for my parents, then in their late seventies, to return permanently to Pennsylvania. They disagreed, partly because the colder winter months aggravated their arthritis, but also, I'm sure, because they could still carry on the Lord's work in Mexico—even if only part time.

Back in Pennsylvania—Truly Retired

Even servants as dedicated as David and Georgina Solt eventually reach a time when they must truly retire. For my parents, that time was—or seemed to be 2003. After a difficult good bye to their many friends in Latin America, Dad and Mom returned to the States and moved in with Liz and Bruce. Then, the day before America's Independence Day in 2004, they moved into a retirement home in Telford. But, even with that move, they still wrote that *"We plan to visit Cancun as the Lord permits."* Sure enough, they returned. In a November 2004 letter, they wrote,

> *We have been here in Cancun since August 10. We continue to repair films and projectors, also offering our help to the radio station. David took trips to the Merida film office once a month for the day. Last month we turned the Merida film office over to the Presbyterian Church so they can run it; therefore, David won't have to make the monthly trip. Our Cancun office will remain in operation as we have a good Mexican manager.*

Then I went there to help them pack for the return trip to Pennsylvania. What follows are my journal entries during that time …

Hurricane Wilma, 2005 (from Lois' Journal from Oct.19-30, 2005)

I asked my husband if I could go to Cancun and help my parents pack up their belongings, as they had retired from the ministry there and were permanently moving to the Lutheran Home in Pennsylvania. Little did we know that God had a hair-raising experience for me and my parents over eleven days. I am glad for the time I had with them alone.

October 19, 2005: We knew a hurricane was coming, but Dad felt that it would be no worse than some other hurricanes that came through Cancun, so he did not prepare.

136

Brother Dave encouraged us to leave the beachfront condo and go into the city before the storm came. Dad said we would stay in our condo.

October 20, Friday:

Dear family,

I am writing this by votive candlelight as the winds howl around us at 140 miles an hour on the ocean side. God has protected us so far. Since the winds were picking up, Dad decided that we would leave. He went down to the borrowed SUV, but it would not start. We were stranded on the beach, with a hurricane bearing down on us!

We were moved to a beautiful condo by the Bellamar guardhouse. Thankfully, the owners had the windows boarded up! We lost our electricity at 2:15 P.M., and water is flooding in all over! This is really tough! Oh, God protect us! The floors are covered in water and I fear for Mom and Dad, walking 20 feet to their bathroom. We have no running water. We know you are all praying for us.

I know that it was no mistake that I came to Mexico. I am now with Mom and Dad through this storm. All of Cancun is inundated, with no area free of water or wind. Dad is always trying to figure out ways to keep the water from coming in through the windows but it is not working. I put in ear plugs to drown out the howling winds.

I remember when our family faced a crisis in El Tapon, Guatemala, when I was almost 14. I asked the Lord to spare my Dad from going over the cliff. I asked Him to let us six kids grow up to adulthood to be a testimony to the world of His faithfulness. I face another terrible crisis with Mom and Dad and pray that God will use this for His glory.

Oh, the poor people of Cancun, Cozumel, and Isla Mujeres! Houses will be washed away. The ocean is flooding over our parking lot. The ocean has taken over. God gave me a Psalm 46; He said, "Be still and know that I am God."

I love you all, Lois, or Mom

October 21, Saturday:

With God's care, ear plugs and sleeping pills, we made it through the night! When mother woke up at 2 A.M., to walk to the bathroom, she found plate glass shattered over the floors and furniture. The plywood covering the windows was coming loose. The winds were incredible. The night before, we played Mexican train dominos by candlelight until 8 P.M. Fortunately for us, we went to bed early because we could not stand the howling winds and the plywood banging! It was while we were asleep that all the glass broke, so praise the Lord, we did not get hurt.

At 5:20 I was awakened by banging on the door. Three security guards stopped by to check on us. Although this was a year-round condominium that Mom and Dad owned, few people were staying in the other beachfront condos at the time. One guard had me look in on my sleeping parents to make sure they were okay.

At 10 A.M. we went to our condo, number 217, only to find the living room completely devastated, with plate glass shattered over everything, and with the windows blown out, the guest bedroom mattress was soaked, as were all the linens. We put important things into their dry bedroom. The guard, Erlin, helped us with moving some towels, water, and food back to condo 308. As we walked down to the first floor we passed many condos with windows blown out, and beds and furniture blown about. We walked across the slippery floor in the reception area and saw the muddy pool. The palapa (straw) grill was blown apart. As we walked up the steps to the third floor we were almost blown off our feet by a gust of wind as we turned the corner. The road in front of Bellamar had become a large, rapidly flowing river. The palms have lost their fronds.

Back at the 308 condo Dad began to re-screw and nail the plywood that had loosened. I helped him, standing in six inches of muddy water on the balcony. At least the wood protected us from the wind and rain. God is here with us and cares for us.

Noon: The second part of the hurricane is now swinging into action. Oh, Lord, when will it end? The wind is coming from the other side and my parent's bedroom has water coming in through the window.

October 22, Sunday: We were up at 6:00 A.M., and we praise the Lord there was no more shattered glass, just water all over the floors. I started to clean up water, an unending job. The wind stopped its ferocious blowing and slowed to eighty miles per hour. Dad worked on the SUV for two hours, trying to get it to start. After it was connected to another car with jumper cables it came to life. We went to the guard house to call missionary Greg Smith and, praise, the Lord we got through and asked him to call Liz and our family in the States.

1 P.M.: Dad wanted to drive to town, but one of the guards stopped him because they knew that there was terrible flooding and looting; police were not allowing people into town. We saw twenty van loads of hotel guests returning to the nearby Costa Real Hotel. They had been in a movie theater in town for three days. The hotel had no running water or electricity.

October 23, Monday: I found a sizeable leak coming through my bathroom light fixture. We had a bucket under it to catch water for flushing the toilets. I thought it looked pretty clean, so I washed my hair, and it sure felt good!

October 24, Tuesday: Airport closed so I could not leave as planned. John did not know what was happening because I could not reach him for four days.

8:30 A.M.: Went to my parents' condo, 217, and started to clean up the water and plate glass. Dad used some plywood we found downstairs to cover the windows. Mom and I worked hard cleaning the kitchen and floors. She is a trooper! Dad is a genius and can

139

improvise to fix anything. He is our famous engineer! Most meals we had bread, an egg, a piece of cheese and sometimes sardines (that someone brought to us).

Noon: We went into the city and saw much devastation along the way. Palm trees, electrical towers, and debris were blown every which way! We went to the film office at the Presbyterian Church to check on the film library and projectors that they use in their ministry. One-hundred-twenty tourists who had been at the Hyatt hotel were bedded down there. At the old house Dad owned the people gave us a five-gallon jug of pure drinking water. Thank you, Lord! We arrived at Greg and Linda Smith's house and learned that their home had gas service, so we baked a frozen pizza we brought, and boiled eighteen eggs. Now we had some more food for the next few days. (Dad wanted to have an Easter Egg hunt tonight!)

We were able to call Pennsylvania, and my sweet John, in Tennessee! I reassured John that we were all doing well. With Dad's help we were able to recharge Greg's palm computer. Their new house, out of town, had suffered major damage, so they were not able to move in the next week. As we drove around town we looked for bread, batteries, and candles, but we were unsuccessful. Fortunately, the guest condo we were using had eight votive candles, which we used. You know, when everything is so dark it is surprising how bright a little votive candle shines. By this example I am reminded that my Christian life shines in this dark land. I was able to witness to four people and gave out two Spanish tracts. We swung by Vacation Club International and saw that water was being handed out. Mother showed her card and both of us got a liter of water, a candle and matches.

October 26: Early in the morning I walked the beach and saw a pelican and blue heron just basking in the sun, sitting on posts, preening themselves—no worries. God said He would take care of the little sparrow, and here I saw birds calmly sitting on their perches.

The airport remains closed. I called Continental Airlines and learned that I'd been pushed from Thursday to Sunday. We found a restaurant open and had some hot soup with tacos—so good! Walmart was open, and we could go into the store in groups of twenty to get water, tortillas, and bananas. Long lines of people were waiting to get in.

October 27, Thursday, 11 A.M.: The lights came on! We have no gas or running water. Our fans and refrigerator are running, but the air conditioners were all turned off to conserve electricity. My left knee is painful and swollen from carrying water from the cistern up to the third floor over and over again. Mother made me rest while they packed up their apartment. Mother' shoulder and back are very sore too, but she plugs along, going through their things, deciding what to keep and what to give away. Thank the Lord for the sun, which is drying out all our bedding and clothing.

October 29, Saturday: The saga continues as many tourists try to get out of Cancun. My parents took me to the airport at 10 A.M. and got a wheelchair, which put me at the front of the line. We were told that the one Continental flight had just left and there would not be another one for four days! I cried. They told me I could get on a bus to Merida (a five-and-a-half-hour drive) and fly out on Sunday to Houston. We decided to do this and we said goodbye to each other. Mom and Dad were scheduled to fly out November 3. (When they did, they were the only ones on the plane!!)

The air conditioned bus was great, but the bathroom had no water. Some areas of the road were washed out, so we had to detour and finally reached the Best Western Hotel that evening. It was good to have a warm shower. I was asked to be translator for the sixty tourists that were on the bus and at the hotel with me.

October 30, Sunday: The next morning we were all up at 4:30 to get to the airport in Merida. I flew to Houston but missed the connecting flight to Nashville, so again tears ran down my cheeks. I finally left at noon, on first class, and made it safely to John at 2:00 P.M. It was good to be home with my husband. I'll never forget this special time with Mother and Dad. We had precious moments sharing stories and thoughts.

Trips to Costa Rica and Zambia

They did return to the retirement home in Telford to live out their final days. But in 2009, they returned to Costa Rica to visit Lillian. On that trip, Mom wrote,

The Nazareth Church had really grown.

We have had three work teams with thirty workers. Some have been coming for twenty-four years. The last five years they have worked on the St. Thomas church and it is nearing completion. We do translation, money changing, and complete any small jobs to save Lillian's time and energy. One week we had VBS with over 100 children from the community. Team members, not knowing Spanish, helped with the crafts and we helped with some of the translation.

Before we arrived, on December 31, Costa Rica had heavy rains with flooding and mudslides. The January 8 earthquake (6.2 Richter) frightened us all since it was a strong shake and lasted a while. Eighteen people died as mudslides buried their homes, with families inside, and farm land, which was their food supply. Bridges and highways were also destroyed, isolating many people. Lillian and Rebeca will be visiting the worst areas with basic supplies. We enjoy listening to TIFC, the radio station we put on the air in 1948. We praise the Lord for the ministry that has continued to this day. The Nazareth Church, which we started with a home Sunday school, celebrated its 50th anniversary last month. The sanctuary has been enlarged to seat 700 in two services.

A very special prayer request for our granddaughter, Joy Miller (Lois' oldest), who is nearing her delivery date. The baby lacks some of the very important organs, and doctors state that he cannot live on his own. This brings much sorrow for all of us. (Praise God, Isaiah was born February 20, 2009, and even with special needs, he is a happy three-year-old today.)

Even as late as 2010, when Mother was 87 and Dad 84, they felt they had one more big trip to take—to Zambia, in Africa! They felt they had to go see John and his wife, Faith. Lillian went along to help them. My parents wanted to visit their youngest son on the foreign field before they died.

Some of us felt that this trip would be very detrimental to their health, but we told them that if God wanted to take them, then what a blessing it would be to go on another mission trip. The day after they arrived, Mother got very sick for three days. Fortunately, Lillian is a nurse and could care for Mother. Dad thought Mom was going to die and he was sorry they had come. Fortunately, she did recover.

John flew them for a short vacation to see Victoria Falls and the animals at Chobe National Park, and to one of the mission stations we support, Macha. He also took them to meet James and Elosia, the village family they lived with for two weeks when they got to the field. James was so sweet in talking with Mom and Dad. He said, *"Since John and Faith are my brother and sister, you are my mom and dad."* So Mom and Dad now have two more children and five more grandchildren.

Mom, Dad, and Lillian visited with John, Faith, and their friends, James and Elosia.

Thousands of Solts

The truth is, I have more brothers and sisters than I can count, because God used my parents to bring untold thousands into His kingdom, and in a sense, each of those many thousands is, spiritually, a Solt child. My natural-born brothers and sisters, as well as our thousands of siblings around the world, are immeasurably blessed by the lives and ministry of David and Georgina Solt.

1997 Retirement Recognition for David and Georgina Solt from the Latin American Mission

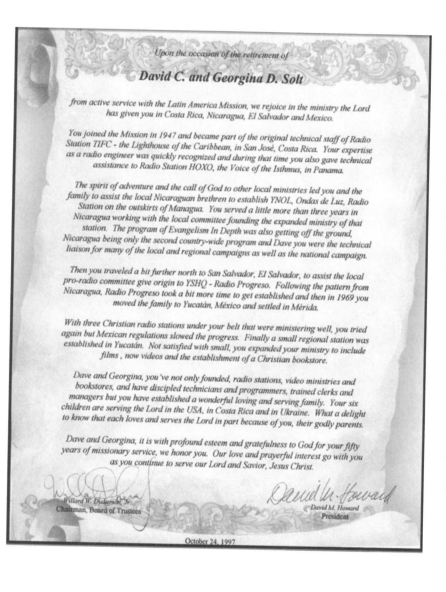

Upon the occasion of the retirement of

David C. and Georgina D. Solt

from active service with the Latin America Mission, we rejoice in the ministry the Lord has given you in Costa Rica, Nicaragua, El Salvador and Mexico.

You joined the Mission in 1947 and became part of the original technical staff of Radio Station TIFC - the Lighthouse of the Caribbean, in San José, Costa Rica. Your expertise as a radio engineer was quickly recognized and during that time you also gave technical assistance to Radio Station HOXO, the Voice of the Isthmus, in Panama.

The spirit of adventure and the call of God to other local ministries led you and the family to assist the local Nicaraguan brethren to establish YNOL, Ondas de Luz, Radio Station on the outskirts of Managua. You served a little more than three years in Nicaragua working with the local committee founding the expanded ministry of that station. The program of Evangelism In Depth was also getting off the ground, Nicaragua being only the second country-wide program and Dave you were the technical liaison for many of the local and regional campaigns as well as the national campaign.

Then you traveled a bit further north to San Salvador, El Salvador, to assist the local pro-radio committee give origin to YSHQ - Radio Progreso. Following the pattern from Nicaragua, Radio Progreso took a bit more time to get established and then in 1969 you moved the family to Yucatán, México and settled in Mérida.

With three Christian radio stations under your belt that were ministering well, you tried again but Mexican regulations slowed the progress. Finally a small regional station was established in Yucatán. Not satisfied with small, you expanded your ministry to include films, now videos and the establishment of a Christian bookstore.

Dave and Georgina, you've not only founded, radio stations, video ministries and bookstores, and have discipled technicians and programmers, trained clerks and managers but you have established a wonderful loving and serving family. Your six children are serving the Lord in the USA, in Costa Rica and in Ukraine. What a delight to know that each loves and serves the Lord in part because of you, their godly parents.

Dave and Georgina, it is with profound esteem and gratefulness to God for your fifty years of missionary service, we honor you. Our love and prayerful interest go with you as you continue to serve our Lord and Savior, Jesus Christ.

Willard W. Dickerson, Jr.
Chairman, Board of Trustees

David M. Howard
President

October 24, 1997

144

Appendices

Lifetime Achievement Award Philadelphia Biblical University,
October 2007

The Solts have been missionaries with the Latin America Mission (LAM) for fifty-nine years. Dr. Solt, an Electrical engineer, graduated from Swarthmore College in 1946 and then attended Philadelphia School of the Bible through 1947. He received both a Master's in Cinematography in 1955 and a Doctorate in Mass Communications in 1971 from Syracuse University. Georgina graduated from PSB in 1947.

Dr. Solt has served as a consultant in radio, television, and mass communications in more than 50 countries. The majority of their work has been in setting up Christian cultural radio stations in Central America and Mexico. They draw up the plans and supervise the construction of the studios, build the towers and transmitter, and train the personnel to run the stations. They have helped to establish eight radio stations, which are locally owned ministries.

For years they taught theological education by extension in many areas of the Yucatan Peninsula. Georgina has written five workbooks for the Mayan Indians in simple Spanish. Her Christian education course has been rewritten with the help of others and is widely used throughout Mexico.

The Solts always work as a team. At one time they had two tents that were used for evangelism and church planting. One tent was large enough to seat 2,000 people. Luis Palau, Billy Graham, Hermano Pablo, and Hyman Appleman were among those who spoke there. During that time the Solts were also involved in distributing 250,000 New Testaments throughout the Yucatan Peninsula, in Mexico.

They also had a film ministry that utilized 350 16-mm projectors. They had more than 500 different Spanish titles, the largest collection in Latin America. Over the twenty-two years, the ministry recorded 97,334 showings, with 8,406,219 viewers and 77,927 decisions for Christ. Many churches were started as a result of this ministry.

The Solts' six children were all born in Central America: Lois '71, Lillian '73, Elizabeth, David, Marc x'79 , and John x'82. Five of their children have served on the mission field at some point in their lives. Elizabeth's house served as our home base in Pennsylvania. She and her husband also helped with all the finances while we were abroad.

David and Georgina also have twenty grandchildren, and six of them have attended PBU. They promised their grandchildren that they would pay for one year of Bible College, a promise of which many of the grandchildren took advantage.

As of 2011, David and Georgina have nine great grandchildren.

Lois Emr, November 2002

My parents have always been an encouragement to me. I was their firstborn, and they have been great parents to me. Some of my siblings may have some other feelings. As difficult as losing my firstborn son, Matthew, was, that painful loss did not compare with losing my husband, Doug Emr, in Ukraine, where we were missionaries. When his heart stopped in a Belaya Tserkov clinic on July 19, 2002, I used a cell phone of one of our students, Igor Solod, to call 5,000 miles away to my sister Liz.

I was all alone, my children in the States and my dear parents far away. My missionary friend, Judy VanSant, in south Ukraine, flew to be with me. She was my comfort, as well as the Bible college students. I flew home with an American who was on a mission trip to help our ministry.

The night before, when Doug was feeling ill, he wanted me to tell some of his special students that he loved them. He broke down and said, "I miss my kids." He said that the only thing he really wanted in life was to be a good father and husband. He also had an outstanding burden to witness for the Lord through creative means in the States, in Mexico, and in Ukraine.

My parents and Lillian flew home from Mexico and Costa Rica to be at the memorial service on July 26. It was so good to be in my mother's arms. My parents wrote to me soon after they returned to Mexico:

"Lois we share your grief, and we are sure as the days go by you will miss Doug more and more. Be assured of our prayers. None of us will understand what you are going through, but God never makes a mistake. It still is like a dream that Doug is with the Lord. 'Precious in the sight of the Lord is the death of his saints.' May God give you the strength and courage to continue. You have four great children. Spend time with them. We are glad that you are not planning to return to Ukraine right away. Love, Mother and Dad."

Is it worth it? After the death of our baby son on January 28, 1974, and the death of my husband, Doug Emr, in July 2002, I have wondered,

"Is it worth it to follow Jesus?" After serving the Lord in cold Ukraine for ten years, is it worth it? Is it worth the pain, the loneliness, the adjustments, the new language, and the criticisms in a foreign country?

Yes! It is worth it all. There are so many new believers that make it worthwhile serving God in Ukraine. At International Baptist Bible College, our students are studying to be pastors and missionaries. Some of these men gave up jobs as engineers and military officers with the KGB to preach the Word of God.

If I had the opportunity to live my life all over again with Doug in the pastorate in Pennsylvania and as a missionary in Ukraine I would do it without hesitation. Being in Ukraine was the most challenging and the most rewarding time of our lives. Doug is now in Heaven with some of the people he led to the Lord! I don't know what the Lord has for me in the future, but I want to serve Him with all my heart and life, wherever He leads me.

**At Thanksgiving, 2002, my children and I flew to Cancun, Mexico, to be with my parents. They provided a place for us to stay in a hotel and helped us with food. It was a good time of healing in a beautiful sunny beach.

God has been good to us, and now all my children are married and I have a kind, loving second husband, Pastor John Blackwell. I am glad that I can continue to serve the Lord in Tennessee and make mission trips to Costa Rica and Ukraine.

Mother and Dad are living in a Lutheran Retirement Community in Telford, Pennsylvania. Over the last five years, they traveled to Los Lagos, Costa Rica, to help Lillian, from January to the end of March (to get out of the cold north). They help her with many of her needs and help her with mission work teams that come to Costa Rica during these months. They also visited their missionary pilot son, John and Faith, in Zambia in 2010.

"San Jose, Costa Rica is where we started our radio ministry, and we have enjoyed celebrating TIFC, 'Lighthouse of the Caribbean's' anniversaries each year, including their sixty-fourth, this year. Our sixty-five-year missionary journey has been a very special blessing of the Lord. Our six children have been an integral part of our missionary ministry, for which we are very grateful. We feel like Hudson Taylor, who stated, "If I had a thousand lives to live, I would offer them all to the Lord." Missionary service has been very enjoyable and rewarding. To God, who made our lives so worth living, be the Glory."

Email: dgsolt@hotmail.com
Georgina's birthday: November 12, 1923
David's birthday: March 17, 1926

Lois Solt Emr Blackwell, RN BS (Birthday 6.15.48)

I attended Grandview Hospital Nursing School in Sellersville, Pennsylvania, and graduated in 1969, with high honors. From there I attended Philadelphia College of Bible for two years, for a BS in Bible, where I met my first husband, Douglas Emr. We married July 3, 1971, and served the Lord in Philadelphia at Memorial Baptist Church for seven years. He worked many years for Prudential between pastoring a church.

After serving at Limerick Chapel in Pennsylvania, we went to Ukraine and started International Baptist Bible College, and eight churches, now led by national pastors. Doug was taken to Heaven on July 19, 2002. We have four children and seven grandchildren. Joy is married to Chris Miller and has two sons. Doug married Sarah Lebo December 2011. Dave and Lori Emr have a daughter and two sons. Our youngest, Dan, and his wife, Stephanie, have a son and daughter. I married Pastor John Blackwell in March 2004, and we serve at First Baptist Church of Ridgetop, Tennessee. John has two children, Andy and Molly, and four grandchildren. I continue to work fulltime in nursing as a certified postanesthesia nurse at North Crest Medical Center in Springfield, Tennessee.

Three sisters celebrated Mother's 85th birthday in Tennessee.

Lillian Ruth Solt, RN BSN (Birthday 12.10.49)

Lillian attended Allentown General Hospital School of Nursing (1969-1971) in Pennsylvania, and Philadelphia College of Bible, where she was granted a BS in Bible in 1973. She also trained as a State Certified Midwife in London, England, and in tropical medicine in Canada, preparing for the life of a nurse in a third-world country. She left for Costa Rica in 1974 as single missionary with Latin America Mission. Even though her marriage to Jose Ramirez ended in deep heartache, Lillian did not give up. She moved forward and helped single moms like herself. She raised her daughter, Rebeca, to know and love the Lord.

She worked in the south of Costa Rica for twenty-five years, sometimes riding horses to get to the remotest parts to teach preventative health, to deliver babies, and to incorporate projects like coffee, bread, medicinal plants and organic gardens that would improve the lives of her friends. Now she oversees CEDCAS, a clinic in Los Lagos, which opened its doors in 2002. The new building was constructed incorporating three houses that Lillian bought over the years. The clinic ministers to the people in the surrounding poor neighborhoods.

Elizabeth Mae Detweiler, RN (Birthday 12.16.50)

Liz (Libet, Lizbeth) married Bruce Detweiler on December 18, 1971, at Bethany Bible Fellowship, Hatfield, Pennsylvania. She graduated from Grand View School of Nursing June 1972, and is a registered nurse. They have three sons: Jonathan, married to Sharon; Joshua, married to Jenny; and Andrew, married to Ashlea. They have three granddaughters.

Her primary goal in life is to be a godly wife and mother. She worked part time as a nurse after two older sons were born. Then she worked for David and John Solt at their engineering firm, Omnitronix, from 1992 to 2002. From 2002 to the present, she has worked as a controller for Detweiler, Hershey and Associates (Bruce's CPA firm) and two other companies. She is active in church, Bible studies, and along with Bruce, she serves on care teams that meet people's needs. They also have opened their home apartment to family members who have been serving overseas. They have watched over extended family finances when we served overseas.

David Lloyd Solt, MBA (Birthday 9.7.53)

 David earned his BS in Electrical Engineering, Syracuse University in 1974; Master of Business Administration, Syracuse University in 1975; Graduate Studies, Westminster Theological Seminary in 1976; MS in Engineering (Electronics), Penn State University in 1982.

He married Pat on June 14, 1975, in New Jersey. They worked under Mission to the World (1985-1987) with a team in Ecuador. They have four children: Ben, Sana (married to Dr. Dustin Donofry), Paul, and Laura.

David started Omnitronix, Inc. (1987 to 2000) and was president/owner, bringing to market the world's first solid-state commercial shortwave transmitter. (He helped place some of his transmitters in Central America and Mexico in Christian radio stations that Dad started.) Valley Forge Scientific Corporation (2000 to 2005): VP of Manufacturing and Research & Development. He was responsible for the development and manufacture of bipolar electrosurgical generators. InfraScan, Inc. (2005 to present): Vice President of Research & Development. He presently is responsible for the development and manufacture of the Infrascanner, a handheld brain hematoma detector that has FDA approval. It is being used around the world to save lives. They are both very active in their church.

Dr. Marc Charles Solt, DMin (Birthday 1.5.58)

Marc attended Philadelphia College of Bible 1975-1977 and transferred to Wheaton College 1977-1979 (graduated with honors); Dallas Theological Seminary 1980-1983 (Masters in Biblical Studies); Trinity Evangelical Divinity School 1989-1993 (Doctorate of Ministry, thesis was on Hispanic Urban Church Planting). He is now the Assistant Director of GATEWAY Theological Institute Training, Evangelical Free Church of America's Director of Development.

He married Colleen Ruth on December 18, 1981. They have five children: Dr. Karisa Schreck, MD/PhD (married to Tom); Tim (married to Ellen), Dan, Caleb and Joshua (twins). Marc has been working with Prudential for 25 years while he has started five Hispanic churches in the Northeast and left them in the hands of Hispanic pastors. He helps to prepare Hispanics to be ministers of the gospel in EFCA churches.

John Jacob Solt, MBA (Birthday 9.17.60)

John was a special student at Philadelphia College of Bible (1978-79); LeTourneau University (BS degree Aviation and Electrical Engineering Technology, 1979-1983); DeSales University (MBA, 2005). He also worked closely with David (1987-1999) in Omnitonix, building solid-state commercial shortwave transmitters.

John married Faith on April 21, 2001, in Harleyville, Pennsylvania. God brought Faith into John's life through a mutual acquaintance. He had heartache in his first marriage, to Lisa, which ended in divorce. Faith also experienced similar heartache through which God's love and mercy were poured out to her. She, too, had an interest in missions. Together, they have five children: Philip, Matthew, Alyssa, Daryl, and Cheri (married to Christopher Maciolek). They have three grandchildren.

Faith knew about John's commitment to be a missionary pilot—he dedicated his life at the age of 15, at Urbana, in Illinois. She wanted to help him fulfill that commitment. From 2004 they started to plan on fulfilling that commitment. On their vacations they would travel to different mission fields to interview. He was employed at Merck in

Pennsylvania, from July 1999 to 2008. He worked as a project engineer and project manager. In January 2009, they left for Zambia under SIM and then were loaned to Flying Missions. He serves as a pilot and mechanic, fulfilling the commitment he made thirty-two years ago.

155

God Uses Imperfect People

Praise the Lord that we all want to serve the Lord in different fields of ministry. We hope that you will put your trust in Jesus Christ. He said, "I am the way, the truth, and the life, no one comes to the Father but by me" (John 14:6). Another verse that we would like to share with you is John 3:16: "For God so loved the world, that He gave his only begotten son, that whosoever believeth in him should not perish but have everlasting life." Through the pages of this book you have seen that we all have flaws and yet a merciful God has chosen to use us. He can do the same for you.

If you would like to contact me, please write to
loisann615@hotmail.com

Special Letters Written to Our Parents or Friends

Here are a few letters that my parents saved over the years.

January 30, 1974 (Letter from Lois to parents, two days after Matthew was stillborn):

Dearest Mother and Dad,

How can we begin but to say we love you. I praise the Lord for the way you taught me to trust the Lord at an early age no matter what the circumstances would be.

I went into false labor on Thursday, Jan 24. I didn't know it was false but when they stopped the next day I went home. Sunday I went in to see if I had dilated. It was Sunday 2 pm and the doc heard a normal fetal heartbeat. X-rays were done to make sure the pelvis was wide enough for the head. We went home to sleep. That night the contractions started to be regular and stronger and we went to the hospital. It was at Jan. 28, Monday, 6 am, and no one could hear the heart beat of our baby but no one panicked as the baby could have been in a posterior position. My labor got harder and I was sedated and taken to have an EEG to try and detect any fetal movement…brain or heart. There was none but they did not tell me. Doug was told that the baby was probably stillborn and he called Pastor Mahurin who came and encouraged him throughout the day.

I delivered at 6:26 pm and heard no cry. Dr. Conrad said to me, "Lois, I guess you know your baby is not alive." I knew but I did not cry. Doug was such an encouragement through labor and delivery to me even though he was agonized with the truth. He went down to Pastor while I got stitched up and when he came back we both wept in each others arms. It is so hard. We loved our baby boy even though we never held him alive. Doug saw him and said he was a beautiful baby weighing 8 lbs and 3 oz. It is so hard not to be able to held the little one you wanted so much to love and train. My arms ached for him. Doug and I have been doing a lot of crying and God is very near to us. We know He loves us more than anybody and he is teaching us more about being like Christ. Our love for each other has deepened.

Doug, Liz, Bruce, Pastor and Mr. Harold Detweiler went with the undertaker to bury Matthew today at 11 am. I sent one of the red roses Doug had given me with a note of my committal of our dear baby back to God. It was a little white casket and was buried in an area where a lot of babies are buried in Leidy church cemetery. Pray for us that we might draw closer to God and be more like Christ.

***

Written January 29, 1974, after talking with me on the phone. Special delivery Mexico to PA. From parents to Lois and Doug

Dearest Loitch and Doug,

How saddened we were to hear the news of your and our baby. So much has happened to you which all seems to be against you, but OUR GOD NEVER MAKES A MISTAKE. How wonderful to know way back at Christmas God was already preparing the way for you to be near your family and friends. This is of special comfort to us.

I know that we can't adequately express in words to you our sympathy and our willingness to try and comfort you. We have been praying for a healthy baby, but God had other plans. It was God who had given you that life and if he chooses to take it back, who are we to question. We know how hard this is for you both. Maybe the Lord is teaching us how to be a comfort to others. We wish so much that we could be with you at this time. You sounded so cheerful on the phone. Praise the Lord! We could hardly talk. All our love to you both!! "Us"

***

Letter from Liz to my parents on Feb 5 (started Jan 29, 1974):

Well by now I know you have heard about Lois and Doug. It was such a shock and many tears were shed. I went to the hospital on Monday night because I felt I was needed. The Lord must have led me because at that time I did not know about the baby. The night supervisor who is a born again Christian told me the baby was stillborn. Then Pastor Mahurin came down to talk to me and he was such a blessing. I spent a ½ hour with Lois and Doug as I had special visiting privileges. Mother and Dad it was so hard to face them. I just hugged Lois and we cried our hearts out. She looked so washed out and really pale-but she still gave a smile and said that she and Doug still had each other. It was so beautiful to see the love expressed between them. Lois said that Doug had really been crying a lot and when I left I hugged him and we shed tears together. The question that went through my mind was, "Lord, why them?" I know that He has his reason. Maybe this will help them in future ministry through the trial.

February 5: I am trying to get over to see Lois and Doug for a short time each day because I know she needs it. They are both doing very well but Lois does become easily depressed. I talked to Lois tonight and she and Doug are going to see a movie. He has been trying so hard to please her and keep her spirits up. He has really done a good job.

***

February 20, 1975 (Letter from Lillian to parents)

Dearest Mother and Dad,

I have been really tired since this month has been so hectic. I was in Honduras helping out in the disaster after hurricane Fifi. Verna is still there working. I think the mental strain of poor communication has been our biggest problem in our organization. I have been with Caravans for a year and things are not going well. We brought up the situation of our being out in the sticks every week this month on different programs such as vaccination, medical caravans of 1,000 people and camps. These commitments had already been made without consulting us so we have to try and fill the obligations. Dita was so upset and she is the most patient person I know. Half way through the meeting she got up and said she resigned. What a blow!! Fortunately Dr. Cabezas and Dr. Bruce were there to back us up.

These past 3 weeks have been very trying to say the least. I have been prayerfully considering what the Lord would have me do when my contract ends in May. On the last Caravan into the bush we saw 930 patients in medicine. After 4 pm we went over to the dental department and started to pull teeth. I would do all the numbing and then Helen and I would start to pull. Dr. Brooke from England just did the fillings. By Friday I was so tired my hands started to cramp every time I gave the Novocain. I appreciate your letters of encouragement so much. Love, Lillian

***

January 31, 1976 (Part of a letter from Liz Detweiler to parents):

Dear Mom and Dad,

As a child I had a lot of sickness and I know I drew a lot of attention but as I grew older I felt apart from the family as my sisters constantly put me down. Today we have all three faced each other and expressed our feelings and forgiven each other. Still at times I feel Lois and Lilly still stand above me and it is a deep hurt. I love them dearly and I love to be especially with Lois but still there is that deep feeling. This was problem that had nothing to do with either of you....sibling rivalry. At times I feel liked Lois is judging Bruce and I, but I know this is how she has been all her life. She tries to correct me like you did Mother when I was at home. I would never trade my sisters for the world because I really love them just as they are. It is still difficult for me to share with them but I am learning thanks to God's patience with me. Mark talked about my inferior complex and I feel this is something that developed through the years of being under Lois and Lilly and feeling like I was less than them. It was very easy for me to turn from them and think only of Bruce because he accepts me just as I am...no additions or subtractions. I always look forward to having Lois here because I feel the way has opened since she lost Matthew...that experience brought us very close.

We love you both dearly,
Liz and Bruce

***

Letter from John to parents July 25, 1982 (John is almost 22 years old, and on a mission trip to Spain)

To My Dearest Parents,

I cannot put into words the love and feelings that I have for you two. You have taught me so much by your examples.

You must understand that God has given me an immeasurable desire to fly. This is part of the reason why I have such a conflict with the military vs mission. I know that the military wouldn't satisfy my needs but nonetheless the feelings are still there. As the Lord leads I will continue the goal of being a missionary pilot. It is a little depressing at time to realize that I will be stuck to a six passenger airplane for that period of time. I always strive for bigger and faster.

I want you to know that my feelings and love for God is a result of your love and prayers for me. I can still remember Mom in San Salvador crying on her bed as she prayed for us children. While I desire to serve God with all my heart I get very discouraged at my weaknesses.

I've always had the challenge and motivation to be someone out of the ordinary. I've never been satisfied being like all the rest. It is also true with my spiritual life. Sometimes I wonder if God will ever use me in the special ways he used His servants in the Old Testament. There is nothing that would mean more to me than the day I stand before His throne to hear: "Well done, my good and faithful servant."

I love you both so very much. You mean so much to me. Thank you for this month that I could be away from all the pressures from back home. I really enjoyed the rest and spiritual fellowship I was able to have in Mallorca, Spain. I'll be praying for you.

His Servant, Love John

(In 2009 John and Faith went to Zambia as missionaries with SIM. John [54 years old] became a missionary bush pilot, the fulfillment of a life-long dream and promise to God.)

***

Letter from Dave and Pat in Ecuador
April 21, 1986

Dear Mother and Dad,

Great news! The twins arrived Wednesday April 9. Their names are Susanna Joy and Paul David. Mom and the twins are fine. Benjamin and Dad are well, and trying to adjust to the stereophonic racket. We have seen God's hand at work in Pat's healthy pregnancy and normal delivery at full term. Because of Benjamin's brush with Crib Death we have the twins on heart monitors until we can have them tested at Children's Hospital in Philadelphia.

We have adjusted well to life here. Our ministry time is exciting. We have a couple Bible studies with the Cristo Vive Church and with young professionals. Last month I gave a seminar on discipleship. It was an excellent time of learning for me as I was able to sift through many of my thoughts on discipleship.

The engineering company I started with four Ecuadorians is going well. God has really opened doors for the business to grow. There are three areas we are working in: computer training for small businesses plus sales and maintenance of small computers. We also do sales and maintenance of electronic medical equipment. This effort takes up all of my non ministry work time.

We love you so much and can now experience first-hand what it was like for you to be on the foreign field as missionaries. Pray for us.

We love you and thank God for you,

Dave and Pat

***

Prayer letter to parents and friends from Lillian, March 1, 1987 (After four years of marriage):

Many of you have not heard from us in many, many months. This has been due to a series of problems which have been very difficult for me to write about. Unfortunately this is one of the most difficult letters I have ever written.

In November, Jose moved out of the house into an apartment. We got together for my birthday Dec. 10. Between counseling, dating and trying to work out some of our differences, a little miracle took place: I got pregnant without knowing it.

My joy was without limit. But I cannot say the same for Jose. Unfortunately, at this time in his life he does not want to have any responsibilities, not as a couple. He gave me two alternatives, abortion or divorce. Obviously I chose the latter. The next day he began the process for divorce and as of last week all of the papers have been signed. My heart is very heavy because much of all of this process has been very difficult for me to accept.

I have met with the Latin America Mission Executive Board and they have been very supportive. I continue to feel the leading of the Lord to work here in Latin America and they are upholding me in this decision. The churches and women with whom we have been working have pleaded with me not to leave Costa Rica which for me has been another indication of the Lord's leading. My sister Lois is going to travel with me in the States to visit my supporting churches.

My prayer is that the Lord will continue to protect the life which I am carrying, that He will give me wisdom and knowledge in raising our baby as a single parent. We need your prayers more than ever today. I love you all dearly and have appreciated your concern, prayers and support over the past years.

In His love, Lillian Solt

(In June Lillian was placed on bed rest. All the stress and tension brought on premature labor. Praise God a beautiful healthy girl, Rebeca, was born on July 22, 1987 by caesarean section. Today Beca is a registered nurse in Costa Rica with her mother in the CEDCAS clinic.)

Letter from Mark to Mother and Dad (sometime in 1986):

I want to thank you from the bottom of my heart for helping me. This is a very difficult time in my life right now, but God is really working. I thank God for the character you built in to me because chances are if I didn't have it I would walk away from my ministry and call it quits. (I'm crying as I write this to you.) It is rather late and I just finished a time of prayer with a foreign student from India. It was a very rich time and once again caused me to question whether I want to stay on the complacent American poster scene. I preach tomorrow night for a Hispanic church.

I have Colleen and Karisa's picture sitting in front of me. They are such a constant source of joy. Colleen is also a real source of strength, support and comfort. She has become my best talking partner. I sure hope God is working in her like He is in me.

All my love,

Your bestest middlest Son, Mark

***

Letter to My Parents
7/13/07 in Tennessee
For 61ST Wedding Anniversary

Dear Mother and Dad,

I'm just in recovery room with a little time on my hands as I wait for another patient....soooo I thought I would thank you both for giving us such a loving family. We are fortunate in that we love each other even if we have differences. You kept our family devotions as a daily priority and now over many years I have also used Our Daily Bread. You gave us adventures that caused our faith to stretch and grow especially on our road trips from PA to Central America: El Tapon, swollen rivers, broken axel, soft, deep shoulder on the road in Guatemala, etc. The diseases we children faced also threw us into prayers of faith: David Lloyd with diphtheria; Liz and Marc with asthma, me with pneumonia, John and the firecrackers that blew up in his pants!

I am so thankful for the life God has given me even though there have been deep "valleys of the shadow of death" which you have prayed me through: Matthew's death January 28, 1974 and Doug's Homegoing on July 19, 2002. God is good even though this life is filled with the effects of sin since Adam. Best of all you led me to a saving knowledge of Jesus when I was very young. God has been at work in my life ever since!

I love you very much and thank the Lord that your love for peoples around the world is passing on to six children, spouses and grandchildren...and hopefully on to the great grandkids.

Happy, Happy Anniversary 61 times.

Love, Lois Ann